the
ultimate
film
guides

Goldfinger

Director
Guy Hamilton

Note by Brian Dunbar

Longman   York Press

York Press
322 Old Brompton Road, London SW5 9JH

Pearson Education Limited
Edinburgh Gate, Harlow, Essex CM20 2JE, United Kingdom
Associated companies, branches and representatives throughout
the world

First published 2001

ISBN 0-582-45249-X

Designed by Vicki Pacey
Phototypeset by Gem Graphics, Trenance, Mawgan Porth, Cornwall
Colour reproduction and film output by Spectrum Colour
Produced by Addison Wesley Longman China Limited, Hong Kong

contents

author of this note Brian Dunbar teaches English and Film Studies at Lasswade High School Centre in Bonnyrigg, Midlothian. He also teaches film courses for the University of Edinburgh's Centre for Continuing Education and is at present Director of Studies for its International Film Studies Summer School.

background

trailer

The incredible, almost impossible plot is carried along from one smashing incident to another and the ability of the more astonishing incidents to provoke admiring laughter as well as chills is a tribute to screenwriting, direction and the stars.

Kinematograph Weekly, 1964

Goldfinger really is a dazzling object lesson in the principle that nothing succeeds like excess.

Monthly Film Bulletin, 1964

Another box-office bonanza for third James Bond film from the Broccoli-Salzman stable; splendidly witty and zestful slice of fantastic hokum, with Sean Connery relishing every dame and fight.

Variety, 1964

The cult of James Bondism is a vicious one, a symptomatic sickness of the age, and the latest in the film series is well in the mould of its predecessors, *Dr No* and *From Russia With Love*. Bondists are expected to shriek with laughter even before the first victim is kicked in the guts or battered against a wall. They must gurgle with relish whenever their nonchalant hero, created by the late Ian Fleming, rolls a girl he's hardly met and certainly hates into the nearest bed. Above all, they must be ready (as soon as they are given the magical wisecrack signal) to roll in the aisles as a man is electrocuted and disintegrates in a flame-coloured flash.

Nina Hibben, The Daily Worker, 16 September 1964

reading goldfinger

'THE NAME'S BOND ... JAMES BOND'

These words instantly conjure up images of sophistication, danger, and sexuality, in plots containing sexy women, memorable villains, gadgets and worldwide conspiracies and, of course, James Bond, a modern-day superman who is every woman's dream and every man's ambition. The release of *Dr No* in 1962 began a series of films which has become the most successful franchise in movie history. Innovative when first released in 1964, *Goldfinger*, like all the Bond films, has become part of an institution, seemingly as much part of Christmas as turkey and cranberry sauce.

As the reviews above demonstrate the film did not meet universal approval, particularly in its depiction of violence and morals. Its attitude to sex and morality was very much in keeping with the times in which great social changes were taking place in Britain, although to today's audiences it does seem somewhat coy. Interestingly *Goldfinger* has very few scenes of violence compared to contemporary action films, and like the sex, it is not graphically portrayed. Gore is not part of the James Bond world. So what, then, is the reason for the continued popularity of the film and the success of the James Bond movies in general?

A major factor in the continued success of the series lies in the series' ability to change with the times without straying too far from the ingredients which first accounted for the films' popularity. The winning formula, whose ingredients can be found in the first two films, was really established with the third film, *Goldfinger*, which also propelled the series to worldwide success.

Of all the Bond films, it is *Goldfinger* which arguably not only created the template for future movies but is also the most perfectly realised of all the films. The self-contained pre-title sequence, the gadgets such as the Aston Martin DB5, the theme song over the titles, the double entendres and humour all become established with *Goldfinger*, and become regular features in later films.

However, the significance of *Goldfinger* goes beyond establishing a winning formula – it reinvigorated the British film industry; established

Sean Connery as an international star; showed the spin-off potential for movies that had rarely been seen before; and influenced the future direction of Hollywood's action thrillers.

Just as importantly the film was part of a British cultural phenomenon which became known as the Swinging Sixties: the emergence of pop culture as a significant economic and cultural force both in Britain and around the world. The Beatlemania of pop music was matched with the release of *Goldfinger*. Incredible scenes at premieres were followed by huge public interest in the film and its stars which was dubbed by the press 'Bondmania'.

Culturally the film coincided with a change in attitudes to morality: the 1950s had seen the rise of John Osborne's angry young man in theatre, and the British New Wave cinema of Lindsay Anderson and others produced gritty realistic films with leading men from the lower classes and accents previously rarely seen in leading roles.

Against this were the James Bond novels of Ian Fleming which created an escapist view of Britain, one which continued with class-conscious views and xenophobic attitudes towards the non-English-speaking world. Fleming's Britain was still a world power for whom the post-war loss of Empire and prestige had never happened. The James Bond of the novels was a snob whose antecedents were the upper-class leading men of the pre-war era, and who increasingly failed to reflect the social changes occurring at the time.

By the time of *Dr No* (1962) the British public were tired of the traditional leading men with their private education, stiff upper lip and class-ridden attitude to life. The casting of Sean Connery with his Scottish accent injected a sense of classlessness into the character at a time when regional accents were becoming more prevalent in films, theatre and other areas of the media. Bond, as exemplified by Connery, gave cinema a new type of hero: the anti-hero; a morally ambiguous protagonist who is on the side of right but whose methods are questionable.

In the 1960s Connery's Bond, with his licence to kill, struck a chord with audiences who were beginning to question established notions of morality. Bond perfectly represented the new permissiveness sweeping the nation.

cinematic influence

Within the films an image of Britain as a major world power was conveyed at a time when Britain was experiencing withdrawal from Empire and endless debates about a new role in the world and angst about her lessened role in world affairs. Fears for the future which arose from this were assuaged by the James Bond films which presented a reassuring view of Britain as not only a major power, but an equal partner of the United States. The reality, of course, was quite different.

In *Goldfinger* it is the USA which is threatened with its gold reserves at Fort Knox being irradiated but it is Bond, representative of Her Majesty's Government, who takes the lead in defeating the villain. Here Bond is the dominant partner in the so-called Special Relationship with his CIA colleague Felix Leiter, indicating that Britain is at least an equal partner with the United States. This reassessment of Britain's position in the world continued in succeeding Bond films, with the UK denying its reduced role in the world by having equal or greater partnership with the USA, USSR and China.

And here we see part of the reason for the success of the films: they managed to project a modern forward-looking view of Britain while at the same time still adhering to traditional values and attitudes.

The cinematic influence of the James Bond films extended beyond Britain. Not only did they inspire countless clones from various countries, they also paved the way for the contemporary action movie while Bond paved the way for other action heroes such as those played by Arnold Schwarzenegger and Bruce Willis. After the success of *Dr No* and then *From Russia With Love* (1963) a bigger budget was assigned to the third film and it is *Goldfinger* which brings together most of the ingredients we associate with the genre: the tough, capable, sexy hero; the array of gadgets; the pre-title sequence; the powerful song; the sexy women; and the memorable sets. And of course the equally memorable set-pieces.

We live in an era when distracted viewing has created a need for films which depend on set-piece scenes rather than plots. The Bond films, particularly *Goldfinger*, helped to establish this trend towards visual spectacle. When thinking of *Goldfinger* who does not immediately think of Connery spread-eagled on a gold table with a laser beam pointed at his genitals? Or Shirley Eaton covered in gold? Or even the golf match between Goldfinger and James Bond? And above all James Bond's Aston Martin DB5, still unsurpassed as the most famous car ever to appear in movies.

SUCCESS OF BOND AND GOLDFINGER

This is based on a number of factors, both cultural, social and cinematic:

■ The image of the UK and the idea of 'Englishness' which appealed to British audiences by bolstering their self-confidence, and to foreign audiences who enjoyed the familiar stereotype of Britain

■ The international plots and glamorous foreign locations appealed to audiences

■ Sex and violence, staples of movie plots since the nineteenth century

■ The film's visual style concealed the fact that the budgets for the early films were not huge but still portrayed a glossy, glamorous expensive look which appealed to audiences beginning to indulge in consumerism

■ Gadgets presenting a vision of the 'near future' fitted perfectly with expectations of the time concerning technological progress and developments leading towards a better future

■ And lastly James Bond himself was a character who not only fitted perfectly with the mood of the times but was, in the mythic sense, a classic hero

BOND AS MYTH

Joseph Campbell in his book *The Hero with a Thousand Faces* (Campbell, 1988), postulates that throughout human history the myths created at different times by different cultures have features and heroes in common. In his book Campbell reduces the diverse myths to one by looking for the common elements: the monomyth. The ingredients of the monomyth are:

■ the hero

■ a summons or call to adventure

■ a quest which separates him from society

quest structure

■ a series of tests and trials in a process of initiation
■ successful completion of tasks
■ successful reintegration into society

The structure of the monomyth will be examined in Narrative & Form. Like many myths *Goldfinger* employs a quest structure.

If we examine Bond then we find that James Bond, the hero, is summoned by M to undertake a quest usually involving the prevention of some global conspiracy in the course of which he is frequently separated from his allies, often in the form of being undercover or captured. Bond is confronted with a number of situations where he has to defeat the villain's forces or extricate himself from dangerous situations. These can be considered tests and trials. When the tasks are successfully completed the villain is defeated and Bond is reintegrated into society. Often this is right at the end of the film when he is literally brought back into society (along with the girl) in the form of a rescue by friendly forces.

The characters who appear in the monomyth are:

■ the hero
■ the villain
■ the princess (maybe someone working for the villain who changes sides; sometimes in a privileged position) who is often rescued from the villain
■ there is a helper who in Bond's case is often Felix Leiter, the CIA operative, or sometimes a girl who works for another intelligence agency
■ lastly there is a wise old man or adviser. This could be M but is just as likely to be Q who equips Bond with the necessary gadgets to help his mission and save his life

A consideration of *Goldfinger* reveals that the broad outlines of the monomyth and its characters are there:

■ the hero, James Bond, is summoned by M, the wise old man, to set out on a quest to find out about the villain, Goldfinger's, gold-smuggling business

■ on the way he is given his gadgets by Q, his adviser

■ Pussy Galore is the princess, or girl in a privileged position, who is rescued from the villain by being persuaded to change sides. After a series of tests and trials during which Bond is almost cut in two by a laser he wins through, kills the villain and gets the princess

■ at the end he is reintegrated into society (after being undercover and isolated for much of the film) when he is rescued by the US

A case can be made for saying that the genre films of cinema are simply contemporary versions of myths which have had their settings and characters brought up to date to make them more relevant to modern society. This can also explain the appeal of the films, since myths attempt to explain those questions which are often unanswerable: our place in the universe, the purpose of life, etc. They also give reassuringly simplistic solutions to problems. Like heroes of old, Bond seems ageless and is there to save us from the dangers which beset us, just as the heroes of old did.

One of the reasons for the success of the films is that they continue to change with the times without losing what are considered to be the essential ingredients. The character of James Bond has been played by five actors (not including the disaster that was *Casino Royale*, 1967). Perhaps that is why Bond does not lose his appeal: every so often a new actor plays the role allowing the character to be ageless, to be relevant to succeeding generations and decades. Like a true mythic hero James Bond is timeless and ageless. And just like these other mythic heroes he is there to solve our problems and assuage our fears.

INFLUENCE OF BOND AND GOLDFINGER

The James Bond films, notably *Goldfinger*, have had an influence on two areas of contemporary cinema: the Hollywood action thriller movie, and what is known as the blockbuster movie.

The characteristics of the modern Hollywood action thriller movie with its emphasis on (usually violent) action over plotting and characterisation; the reduction of narrative complexity to a series of set pieces and chases; the foregrounding of technology and firepower and perhaps, above all, the blockbuster movie

hero who never dispatches a villain without a 'witty' one-liner – can all be traced back to the Bond films, particularly *Goldfinger*. It could be argued that the starring vehicles of Hollywood stars such as Mel Gibson, Arnold Schwarzenegger and Bruce Willis are simply Americanised reworkings of the James Bond formula. The *Indiana Jones* films can also be considered a variant. All the films in this genre are structured around set pieces, designed for spectacle rather than plot to make them instantly appealing to a global audience and their distracted viewing habits.

The modern blockbuster movie, which is commonly held to begin with *Jaws* (1975), can be traced back to *Goldfinger*. All the ingredients are in place with that movie, particularly the turning of the film's release into an event by giving the film a simultaneous release on hundreds of cinema screens. The marketing potential of films was also realised with *Goldfinger*, and, long before *Star Wars* (1977), the Bond films were the subject of licensed merchandise and soundtrack albums. The intention, common now, was to attract a global audience by concentrating on the visual impact of the film over plot.

key players' biographies

SEAN CONNERY

Born Thomas Sean Connery, in 1930, in Edinburgh. He had various jobs including lifeguard and coffin polisher. After representing Scotland in the 1950 Mr Universe contest Connery gained a part in the London chorus of *South Pacific*. Stage, TV and small film parts followed until in 1962 he landed the part of James Bond in *Dr No*, which catapulted him to superstardom. Other Bond films followed: *From Russia With Love*, *Goldfinger*, *Thunderball*, *You Only Live Twice*, *Diamonds are Forever*, and finally a remake of *Thunderball* – *Never Say Never Again*.

In other films Connery tried to move away from the Bond image, preferring to act without his toupee. *The Hill* (1965) was a notable effort to show his acting skills. Connery won an Academy award for Best Supporting Actor in *The Untouchables* (1987) after which he became one of the most sought-after actors in Hollywood and perennial favourite for the world's sexiest man.

GUY HAMILTON

Born in 1922 in Paris to British parents. He was assistant director on classic films such as *The Third Man* (1949) and *The African Queen* (1951). Hamilton is considered a journeyman director who can follow instructions and work efficiently within formulas and generic conventions rather than an auteur. As such he suited the James Bond series where he could follow on from Terence Young. He also directed Connery in *Diamonds are Forever*, and later Roger Moore as Bond in *Live and Let Die* (1973), and *The Man with the Golden Gun* (1974). An interesting film to compare with his Bond work is *Funeral in Berlin* (1966), in which Caine plays Harry Palmer, a character who presented a more realistic antidote to the escapist fantasies of Bond.

KEN ADAM

Born Klaus Adam in 1921 in Berlin. Worked twice for Broccoli's Warwick Pictures – *In the Nick* (1959) and *The Trials of Oscar Wilde* (1960). Adam's sets are marked by clever use of light and perspective as well as strong architectural shapes and forms. The influence of German Expressionism is present. Adam wanted the sets to embody the fantastic, non-realistic nature of the films. In designing the sets it was important to give them a larger-than-life feel to reflect the escapist, fantastical nature of the films. Adam's sets gave *Goldfinger* a feel of the future just around the corner, which was part of the film's success. Additionally, Adam's work is noted for being stylish, inventive and containing a sense of humour, all features which became typical of the James Bond style.

Adam designed the sets for seven Bond films. He did not work on *From Russia With Love*, hence the different look to that film compared to its predecessor *Dr No* and its successor *Goldfinger*. Another example of the modernist larger-than-life sets that Adam became renowned for on Bond is the War Room in Stanley Kubrick's *Dr Strangelove* (1963), the film which prevented him working on *From Russia With Love*. A more recent film which demonstrates his skill as production designer is *Addams Family Values* (1993). Adam won Oscars for *Barry Lyndon* (1975) and *The Madness of King George* (1994).

Eon Productions

GERT FROBE

Born in Germany in 1913, died in 1988. He entered films in 1948, often playing 'heavies'. An actor who could dominate a scene, he unfortunately knew no English when cast as *Goldfinger*. His voice was dubbed by British actor Michael Collins.

HONOR BLACKMAN

Born in 1926. In the early 1960s played Cathy Gale in the TV series *The Avengers*. Her character's independent, tough proto-feminist portrayal in that series led to the role of Pussy Galore where her TV character's skill with unarmed combat was utilised for the film. She continued to have a successful career in films, television and on the stage.

CUBBY BROCCOLI

Born: Albert Romolo 'Cubby' Broccoli in 1909, died in 1997. After moving to Hollywood, Broccoli landed a job as a 'gofer' on Howard Hughes' film, *The Outlaw* (1943). Later he became a production assistant at 20th Century Fox. After the Second World War Broccoli teamed up with Irving Allen and established a production company, Warwick Pictures, in London to take advantage of the Eady subsidies which were awarded to film companies employing British artists. The films produced by the company were very successful and a number of people who would work on the Bond films began with Broccoli at Warwick Pictures, including cinematographer Ted Moore, screenwriter Richard Maibaum, and production designer Ken Adam.

After Broccoli split from Allen, who did not share his enthusiasm for wanting to film the Bond books, he met with Harry Salzman who had an option on the Bond novels but needed a production deal. A deal was struck, and the resulting partnership was named Eon Productions (Everything Or Nothing). Together the two co-produced eight films. When Salzman left the partnership in 1976 Broccoli produced the next four himself before co-producing with stepson Michael G. Wilson and later with his daughter Barbara Broccoli who took his place when he died in 1997.

HARRY SALZMAN

Born in Canada in 1915, died in 1994. He began his film career in England by forming Woodfall Productions with playwright John Osborne and director Tony Richardson. Salzman acquired the option on seven Bond novels and with twenty-eight days left on the option met with Broccoli and agreed to go into partnership to film the books. Unlike Broccoli, Salzman had other interests and also acquired the rights to Len Deighton's novels about spy Harry Palmer, producing three films. Eventually he sold his interest in Eon Productions to United Artists.

JOHN BARRY

Born J.B. Prendergast in 1933 in England. Composer whose arrangement of the Monty Norman theme music has become one of the most recognisable tunes in the world. After two instrumental hit records for United Artists, the film arm of the company employed him to give Monty Norman's theme music an upbeat arrangement. From there Barry went on to score the music for eleven Bond movies. Barry has won Academy Awards for his scores four times: *Born Free* (1966), *The Lion in Winter* (1968), *Out of Africa* (1985), and *Dances with Wolves* (1991).

PETER HUNT

Born in 1928 in London. Edited the first five Bond films before turning to directing. Directed the Bond movie, *On Her Majesty's Secret Service* (1969). Hunt's editing style contributed to the slick nature of the Bond movies.

RICHARD MAIBAUM

Born in New York in 1909, died in 1991. Maibaum wrote or co-wrote every Albert Broccoli-produced Bond film with the exception of *You Only Live Twice*, *Live and Let Die*, and *Moonraker* (1979). Maibaum had previously worked for Broccoli at Warwick Pictures.

PAUL DEHN

Born in Manchester, England in 1912, died in 1976. Co-wrote *Goldfinger* with Richard Maibaum. Later went on to write four sequels for the *Planet of the Apes* series.

biographies

overall responsibility

TED MOORE

Born in South Africa in 1914. Flew for the RAF in the Second World War and was decorated for bravery. Worked as a camera operator on *The African Queen* and *Genevieve* (1953). In the 1960s he became one of Britain's most respected colour and widescreen cinematographers, photographing seven Bond films in total. He won an Academy award for cinematography of *A Man for All Seasons* (1966).

director as auteur

Just as poets, novelists and artists are considered the authors of their work – auteurs – so in film there has been a tendency to seek an author for films: the person responsible for putting the film on screen. In truth there is no one person. Unlike most other art forms, film is the product of the collaboration of many people – director, screenwriter, producer, actors, set designers and editors to name only a few. Also, in mainstream cinema the film makers may be working within a particular genre which will impose certain restrictions and expectations. By the time of *Goldfinger* a formula and style was emerging which militated against an auteur and in favour of directors who could work within the formula and on budget while still bringing some ideas of their own.

The term auteur owes its origins to young French film enthusiasts who wrote for the magazine founded by André Bazin, *Cahiers du Cinema*, in the 1950s. People such as François Truffaut and Jean-Luc Godard sought to elevate the US films they so loved to the same status as other art forms and since in these other forms the status of the art rests principally with the author or artist or composer, they took for their authors the director. This theory they named *politique des auteurs* which was Anglicised in the early 1960s by American film critic Andrew Sarris as the auteur theory.

It is one of the ironies of film making that the person responsible for the detailed plots and dialogue – the screenwriter – is not accorded the same status as in the theatre.

In film making the screenplay is only the beginning: it has to be visualised and this is the work of the director who has the overall responsibility for transferring the screenplay to the screen so this made the director the obvious person to be the auteur. Thus, in the pages of *Cahiers du Cinema* it was directors like John Ford and Alfred Hitchcock who became feted as auteurs. However, not every director is an auteur: there are factors which militate against this e.g. studio influence, the demands of the genre, the stars and their images. Indeed, in the 1930s and 1940s many Hollywood studios had recognisable styles: MGM had its lush extravagant production values; Universal had its expressionist-influenced horror movies; and Warner Bros. had harsh, gritty realism and social comment.

Also in the 1930s and 1940s producers exerted great artistic influence. David O. Selznick is the auteur usually associated with *Gone With The Wind*, not the director, Victor Fleming. In the last twenty years when the director as auteur has been used as a marketing device to sell films, producers such as Don Simpson (for example, *Top Gun*, 1986) can be considered auteurs; although he did not direct any films, as producer he had control over all aspects of his films and was certainly the vision behind his products.

When examining *Goldfinger* and other Bond films the role of the producers Albert Broccoli and Harry Salzman is pivotal in creating both image and style. It is said that Broccoli was the one concerned with lots of glamorous women in the films while Salzman was more interested in the gadgetry, together two of the defining features of the James Bond genre. In addition one should not forget that the films were adapted from the successful novels of Ian Fleming and so this would put certain restrictions on the portrayal of the character of Bond, as well as the interpretation of the books, since there would be a ready-made audience for the films. That is not to say that changes were not made but in general the films kept to the spirit of the novels and characters.

Nevertheless, the most commonly accepted person as auteur is the director, simply because his/her role of being in overall control of the film-making process allows greater freedom and influence. For directors such as John Ford with his westerns and Alfred Hitchcock with his thrillers, the notion of auteur is not unreasonable since their films display a continuity of style and theme and purpose.

For a director to be considered an auteur, therefore, it has to be shown that humorous content

this person has the overriding vision and control to carry it out. If the person has a number of films to his/her credit then, apart from the amount of control exercised, one should also examine the films for preoccupations, themes and style to see if this vision is carried on from film to film. If so, then there is a greater likelihood that the director can be considered an auteur.

Of course, the collective, industrial nature of the film-making process, the star system, and the reliance on genre, all work against the auteur theory. On the other hand many directors choose to construct a team which will work together on a number of films.

In addition, a director-auteur will often choose very carefully the cinematographer for their films. Many great film-maker auteurs have had great cinematographers e.g. Charles Chaplin had Rollie Totheroh, D.W. Griffith had Billy Bitzer, Orson Welles had Gregg Toland who arguably is as much the author of *Citizen Kane* as Welles. Toland taught the young Welles the art of film making and also had to turn Welles' suggestions and requests about types of shots and lighting into reality. In *Citizen Kane*, too, the screenwriter Joseph L. Mankiewicz is often considered as much the author of the film as Orson Welles.

By the beginning of the 1970s new approaches to film analysis such as Marxism, semiology and structuralism which put the emphasis on film as text caused the demise of the auteur theory although it has been rehabilitated with the poststructuralists. Nowadays, the director as auteur is seen as one who has an overriding vision and control. For many film critics and students the director is a logical point of departure when beginning any study of a film's worth.

Goldfinger, like all the James Bond films, cannot be considered as the work of an auteur director. Certainly certain directors, notably Terence Young and Guy Hamilton, have had considerable influence in the formula. Young, as director of the first two films, established the early look of the films but Guy Hamilton, in *Goldfinger*, successfully blended the action of the first two with greater humorous content, as well as bringing the famous gadgets to the fore. Also Hamilton was known for giving his films a glossy look which fitted with the required style of the film. Nevertheless a

Bond formula

comparison between *Goldfinger* and the next film, *Thunderball*, directed by Terence Young, would show great similarities between them, so much so that it would be very difficult to distinguish, between the two, the work of different directors.

However, the success of *Goldfinger* was due to the collaboration of a number of people including director, writers, producers, set designer, composer and its star. These people created a winning formula which remained the model for later films with a few changes here and there. For the Bond films, such as *Goldfinger*, it can be argued that the most important people involved in creating the formula and style were the producers Albert 'Cubby' Broccoli and Harry Salzman, and the production designer Ken Adam whose modernist sets are largely responsible for the look of the film.

Like many auteur directors the producers Broccoli and Salzman gathered together a team which worked on a number of the Bond films. Apart from Ken Adam there was the cinematographer Ted Moore and screenwriter Richard Maibaum who had both worked with Broccoli on Warwick Pictures; editor Peter Hunt and John Barry who scored the soundtrack for eleven films and the famous arrangement of the James Bond theme. Eventually the term 'Bondian' was coined by Broccoli to describe the formula used to make a successful Bond movie, and it is this formula which takes precedence over the demands of any auteur director. A director may bring various strengths and interests to the film but he still has to conform to the formula.

Goldfinger, then, can be seen as a collaborative effort whereby the initial inspiration for the approach to the film and its predecessors comes from the producers who made it clear how they interpreted the character of Bond. Ken Adam's sets gave the films their distinctive appearance while the scriptwriters were responsible for the one-liners and witty dialogue, although Guy Hamilton had an input here as well. John Barry's arrangement of the theme tune is another integral part. And last, but not least, Connery's interpretation of the character was a massive influence on the films.

narrative & form

classical narration

Film can be divided into two main forms: fiction and non-fiction. The vast majority are fiction or narrative films. According to David Bordwell the main form of storytelling which emerged in the sound era after 1930 was Classical Narration, or Hollywood Narration after the United States' dominance of world commercial cinema. This form of film making has storytelling as the principal aim with all other features subordinate to this.

Bordwell identifies a number of features which define Classical Narration. Narrative itself consists of plot and style, where plot refers to the order in which events are seen on screen, and style refers to the film techniques which put the plot on screen. Classical Narration had its heyday between 1930 and 1949. It had practical advantages as it made for quick and efficient film making in an era when cinema-going was the dominant form of entertainment and studios were making movies in vast numbers.

However by 1950 a number of significant changes were beginning to occur. One of these was the break-up of vertical integration, whereby the studios not only controlled the production of films but also, through their parent companies, controlled the distribution networks and cinema chains. Other forms of mass entertainment, such as television, and the growing power of star actors also influenced these changes, although it continued to be a dominating factor until the early 1960s.

Goldfinger was made at a time when the studio system had collapsed and the features of Classical Narration were being loosened. Most mainstream films still conform to the features of Classical Narration although style has assumed increasingly greater importance and can be as important, or even more important, than the plot. An examination of *Goldfinger* reveals that the style employed in the film, and subsequent Bond films, is what people

consequences of actions

associate with a James Bond movie. The plots may be similar from film to film and other films may have similar plots but it is the style of the film which marks the James Bond movies from other action thrillers.

In Classical Narration the end of the film should see all the problems faced by the protagonist resolved. The climactic confrontation in Fort Knox sees Bond foil Goldfinger's plans by neutralising the nuclear device, killing Oddjob his henchman and causing Goldfinger to flee. However there are two resolutions. After thwarting his plans, Bond still has to deal with Goldfinger and win the girl, in this case Pussy Galore. Resolution only truly comes in a Bond movie when he has seduced the girl at the end.

FEATURES OF CLASSICAL NARRATION

■ Storytelling as a main purpose. Films can have a variety of aims: to spread propaganda; to question the society in which we live; to draw attention to the constructed nature of film and society; or simply to entertain. In Classical Narration the purpose is to tell a story; and the plot in this film concerns James Bond's attempts to thwart the villainous Goldfinger's efforts to irradiate the gold of Fort Knox, thereby causing the collapse of the US economy to the benefit of China.

■ Verisimilitude. Films had to present an 'illusion of reality' to audiences, and a number of features contributed to this, particularly the unobtrusive use of film techniques. *Goldfinger* presents a recognisably real world of characters and settings, albeit glamorous and larger-than-life with some improbable, but still recognisable, characters. The world of *Goldfinger* is one in which glamorous individuals and larger-than-life figures exist, while the lives of ordinary people are largely non-existent.

■ Narrative as cause and effect. The events on screen do not exist in isolation. Events interact and future events are influenced by previous events and this gives a linear structure to films. For instance, the killing of Jill Masterson is entirely due to her disobeying Goldfinger and siding with Bond. Similarly, the death of her sister, Tilly, is the consequence of Tilly's attempts to kill Goldfinger and avenge her sister's death.

There are numerous references to the consequences of actions: we are told

effect on individuals

that there is an ejector seat in Bond's DB5. When it is operated later we are expecting it and realise it is the outcome of Q's briefing. Likewise when Bond tells Pussy Galore that to use a pistol in an aeroplane would result in the plane depressurising we are prepared for the finale when Goldfinger fires his revolver which breaks a window, depressurises the cabin and causes him to be sucked out. In Classical Narration each scene serves a purpose: either to further the audience's understanding of the plot, or to prepare the audience for what happens in a later scene.

■ Clearly defined individuals. The characters on screen should have readily identifiable character traits for the audience to identify and empathise with, and the course of the film is determined by individual actions rather than, for instance, social forces. However, the character traits will be those that are considered important to our understanding of the plot or character's role in the plot. For instance, it is not in the film's interests to portray Goldfinger sympathetically at any time as that would complicate our reactions to events. Thus the films like many others rely on stereotyping.

Events are always portrayed in relation to their effect on individuals. We follow Bond, the protagonist, as he seeks to thwart the attempts of the villain to lay waste to America's gold reserves. The outcome is entirely dependent on the efforts of Bond. In addition the characters are clearly defined, exhibiting features which convey the characters' personalities and are relevant to the plot. For instance, early on in the film there is a scene in Miami where Bond catches Goldfinger cheating at cards; this not only tells us that Goldfinger is a cheat and a crook but its narrative function sets the scene for a later dramatic confrontation between Bond and Goldfinger, as well as the ruthless death of Jill Masterson. Similarly the same scene's representation of Bond confirms his 'ladies man' status. The pre-titles sequence indicates to us that Bond is a man of action, cool under pressure, violent when need be, a womaniser, wise-cracking and ruthless.

A major part of defining individuals is their appearance: Bond himself is rarely seen without his carefully tailored suit or tuxedo, indicating his sophistication, style and elitism – he is part of the Establishment (for more on this see Representation).

■ Limited stylistic features. In Classical Narration plot takes precedence over style. Film techniques are designed to be 'invisible', they should convey information to the audience to help it follow and understand the plot but not be intrusive. Among the deliberately limited number of film techniques employed is continuity editing which was designed to facilitate the smooth unfolding of events. A typical set-up would be an **establishing shot** where the particular characters in a scene would be shown in relation to one another then there would be cuts to close-ups of the individuals as they conversed. The meeting of Goldfinger and Bond at the golf course is a case in point, an establishing shot places both characters in the frame before cutting to close-ups. A film should be able to involve an audience in the events on screen, make it easy for these to be followed and the connections between them identified.

■ Resolution. With Classical Narration, plot strands have to be tied up by the end of the film, relationships between characters resolved and equilibrium restored (see Narrative Resolution).

non-linear structures

As discussed above, all plots will have a linear structure in a cause-effect relationship but within this there may be other more general patterns dictated by other structural devices. A three-part structure has emerged in narrative films and other forms of storytelling and is the principal form in Classical Narration, but other devices can be found which are dictated by genre and theme.

While the principal structuring device is cause and effect – whereby every action has a reason and an effect on later events, and the principal character is advanced towards a goal or goals – in narrative films this is often reduced to a simpler overall structure which can be described as:

■ equilibrium
■ disruption
■ restoration of equilibrium

This structure begins with an introduction to the main characters whose

three-part structure

lives are disrupted by an event: for example, a murder, the arrival of a particular character, etc. This creates problems which have to be resolved before the end of the film, by which time, the disruption being eliminated, the characters can return to equilibrium.

The first part of the film is designed to inform us of the plot and introduce the main characters to us, as well as giving us any information which may be necessary to understand the characters' motivations and actions.

Goldfinger conforms broadly to the three-part structure described above. Normality, or equilibrium is when we see Bond in the pre-titles sequence on a mission, destroying a Latin American drug-smuggling operation, his everyday work. This equilibrium continues when he is holidaying in Miami, attracting the company of beautiful girls such as Dink the masseuse, and continues until he is given his mission by a CIA colleague on behalf of M to investigate Goldfinger's gold-smuggling efforts. This then is the disruption and it is at this point that the main problem is revealed: to thwart Goldfinger. All the other problems which arise are a result of Bond taking on this mission, including foiling the plan to irradiate US gold supplies, and escape from death by laser.

When Bond is victorious we have a return to equilibrium, as signified by defusing the atomic device in Fort Knox, then killing Goldfinger and lastly, but certainly not least in the world of James Bond, the successful seduction of Pussy Galore. For Bond, the final scene where he is intimate with the major female character is the real indicator of return to equilibrium. Until this happens audiences do not consider that the film has ended.

GENRE AS STRUCTURING DEVICE

Within the three-part structure more complex patterns can be constructed. Indeed, it is an indicator of genre that certain structures can be specific to particular genres. In addition narrative resolutions are often genre-specific: westerns tend towards shootouts, musicals often end on a big set-piece song-and-dance number, horror movies have the monster successfully confronted by the protagonist, and James Bond films have Bond defeat the villain then win the girl.

However an examination of *Goldfinger* and subsequent Bond movies reveals that this three-part structure is only one structure operating in the film. Genre operates on variation and repetition with repeated features having to be presented in familiar but different ways. Within *Goldfinger* there are structural features which have been retained in subsequent Bond films. The film itself is structured very specifically: first by the gun barrel sequence, then the self-contained pre-titles sequence, the film proper which conforms to the traditional three-part structure, then the final pre-credits sequence. This structure is common to all Bond movies and is one of the indicators of the Bond genre.

GUN BARREL

Designed by Maurice Binder, the film opens with a point-of-view shot which sees the audience staring through a gun barrel, the rifling clearly present to inform us what the tube is. A man, presumed to be Bond walks in front, turns and fires, whereupon the white barrel progressively changes to red from the top, indicating blood, then the barrel shakes. At this point it is clear that the enemy who is pointing the gun has been shot and killed by Bond.

The sequence, first introduced in *Dr No*, has become a trademark for the films and indicates the violence inherent in the films, who the main character is and his deadliness to enemies. The character of Bond here was not played by Sean Connery but by stunt man Bob Simmons. Future actors playing Bond did their version of this scene to convey to the audience the identity of the person playing Bond.

OPENING

Following on from the gun barrel sequence is the pre-titles sequence which is self-contained and has no narrative function within the film. Its purpose is to set up certain expectations about the rest of the film from the character of Bond to the use of violence, sex and witty one-liners, and also the proliferation of gadgets and technology, not necessarily serious. The sequence opens at night with a seagull swimming on the surface of the water only to rise up to reveal it is a snorkel attached to Bond's head. Right away the film signals the foregrounding of technology and its tongue-in-cheek approach.

Moving swiftly but quietly to a series of oil tanks Bond enters by a secret door and finds a store of drugs to which he attaches plastic explosives. The film set is modernist and expressionist, giving a foretaste of those to follow. So far Bond's stock in trade as spy or adventurer is established. After planting the explosives Bond unzips his wetsuit to reveal a white tuxedo and black bow-tie. He then fits a red carnation into his buttonhole.

Not only does this mark Bond out as the coolest person ever in film history, it firmly establishes the humorous nature of the film which both invites us to be impressed at Bond's coolness but also invites us to laugh at the outrageousness of it all. The seagull snorkel and the dancing girl also signal two of the film's defining features – gadgets and girls.

At once the film's intentions are clear; this is not a serious movie and any feature which the audience might find hard to accept is treated in a way which demands laughter from the audience, as if the film makers are colluding with us in agreeing that the film and the character are not to be taken seriously.

This approach continues when Bond goes to a bodego – the drug stash is somewhere in Latin America – and goes upstairs with a dancer. It is a set-up but the sequence shows Bond's resourcefulness: he sees his attacker reflected in the eye of the girl in his arms; he turns her round to take the brunt of the attack, then defeats the attacker by throwing an electric fire in to the bath where he has fallen. Any shock (no pun intended) at what has happened is dissipated when he says, 'Shocking. Positively shocking.'

The witty one-liner is a foretaste of what is to come, both in the film and the series, and again detracts from any criticism of the scene. In the pre-titles sequence the film makers are telling us: it's just escapist entertainment, don't take it seriously.

THE TITLES SEQUENCE
Another trademark of a James Bond movie is the titles sequence where the theme song is sung over images of beautiful girls. Here the girl who

plays the Miami masseuse Dink, Margaret Nolan, is covered in gold while images of the movie are projected on to her body. Again, the nature of the film is foregrounded to the audience. The song, written by John Barry with lyrics by Leslie Bricusse and Anthony Newley, is sung by Shirley Bassey in suitably melodramatic fashion reflecting the dramatic nature of the plot and the villain. The titles sequence was designed by Robert Brownjohn who also designed the titles for *From Russia With Love*, although Maurice Binder is most associated with these sequences, having designed fifteen of them.

narrative resolution

The film's climax comes in a battle inside Fort Knox between Bond and Goldfinger's 'manservant' Oddjob. It is a sequence which becomes typical of later films: a confrontation between villain or henchman in a memorable, unusual location. Once again electrocution is Bond's chosen method of killing. In keeping with the theme of gold, gold bars are used as weapons as well as Oddjob's steel-brimmed hat which has already killed Tilly Masterson. The climax here has been set up earlier in previous scenes featuring Bond and Oddjob.

At this point the danger is still to be averted, namely neutralising the nuclear device. As it is set on a countdown a sense of urgency is injected into the climax to make the scene more dramatic. Again the seriousness of the situation is diluted with humour when Bond, at a loss what to do, is about to pull a wire at random when a hand appears in shot and flicks a switch. The counter on the clock is stopped with seven seconds left – 007 – adding a final joke to the sequence.

The closing sequence begins with a victorious Bond being congratulated by Leiter and a General on behalf of the president. Here we see Bond as saviour of the West, not just of Britain, and it gives greater importance to Britain as the partner of the USA.

When he boards the plane which is piloted by Pussy Galore, we find that Goldfinger, who escaped from Fort Knox, is on the plane intending to take his revenge. After a struggle Goldfinger fires a shot which blows out a window, depressurising the cabin, about which we have been forewarned. Goldfinger is sucked out of the tiny aperture to die a bizarre death, another trademark of the series. It is only left for Bond to take command of the situation when Pussy panics, asserting male superiority over the female. The last scene has Bond and Pussy, having parachuted to safety, hiding from their rescuers under the parachute where it is assumed they make love.

Now the film can end properly, and more importantly, the audience knows the film is at an end since not only is the film's villain defeated but Bond has also successfully seduced the girl, his reward for victory. In the world of James Bond, women function as trophies.

However, there are also other scenes which audiences would expect in a James Bond film and which occur in *Goldfinger*:

■ Bond introducing himself: 'Bond ... James Bond'

■ Bond being given his mission by M (initially through CIA colleague Felix Leiter)

■ Bond flirting with Miss Moneypenny

■ Bond being given his latest gadgets by Q

■ Bond in a dangerous, life-threatening and often bizarre situation

■ Bond being told of the villain's plans

■ Final confrontation with the villain, and the foiling of the villain's plans, often involving a countdown

■ In addition there are spectacular special effects sequences interspersed throughout the film

The need to include these sequences influences the structure of the film since these sequences can only come at certain moments within it. For example, Bond will be given his mission before he meets Q for his special weapons. Additionally the obligatory flirting with Moneypenny can come directly before or after his briefing by M but has to be in the same part of the film. At some point Bond will introduce himself with the words

'Bond ... James Bond'. In the first film, *Dr No*, this happened very early on as a way of indicating to audiences as well as characters who he was. Later films kept the line although it now functions more as a generic feature than narrative information. It has become part of the expectations of the audience, just like 'shaken, not stirred'.

Additionally, as we shall see in Contexts, the James Bond movies have their antecedents in older genres, one of which is the old cliffhanger serial which was structured around moments of great suspense every fifteen minutes. Similarly Bond films are structured around a number of set-pieces: *Goldfinger* has the death of Jill Masterson by being painted gold; the golf match; the car chase leading to Bond's brush with the laser; Goldfinger's explanation of his plan to the gangsters; and the attack on Fort Knox. This type of structure based on the need for a set piece or a special effects action sequence is not only indicative of the James Bond movies but also most contemporary action thrillers.

MYTH AND FAIRY TALE STRUCTURE

As mentioned in Background, James Bond can be seen as a mythic hero, like King Arthur or those heroes of ancient Greece. The basic structure found in myths is the quest. Again, *Goldfinger* and other Bond films conform to this.

The quest structure involves the hero being called to adventure, receiving advice and then setting out to seek the object of the quest, defeating wrong-doers or anyone who stands in his way before returning to society. In *Goldfinger* Bond's mission functions as the quest, while M and Q are the wise old men or advisers. The successful completion of the quest, which is the defeat of Goldfinger, allows Bond to return to society. This is signified by his getting the girl and being rescued by friendly forces, who represent society.

GOLDFINGER AS OEDIPAL TRAJECTORY

The psychoanalytical term 'Oedipal trajectory', when applied to film, refers to the classical narration convention whereby the male protagonist successfully solves the problems and, at the resolution of the film, achieves social stability. This basically means that he gets the girl and settles down. In *Goldfinger*, and other Bond movies, the hero gets the girl but the convention of the genre is that the relationship we see at the end will not necessarily continue. Bond after all is a hero for the 1960s where sexual relationships became more casual.

The fact that Bond can be analysed in psychoanalytic terms is understood by the film makers who make humorous references to this. For example, in the pre-titles sequence there is a reference to the size of Bond's gun being connected to his inferiority complex. This is a thinly veiled allusion to the size of his penis, and draws attention to psychoanalysts' habit of finding phallic objects in movies and relating them to male sexual fears. The fear of castration, another psychoanalytic preoccupation is alluded to when Bond is strapped to the gold-topped table in Goldfinger's factory and a laser beam is slowly but surely progressing along the table and up his legs.

structural oppositions

Films can also be structured according to oppositions found in the films; in *Goldfinger* these are between characters and opposing ideologies. First of all there are a number of oppositions relating to the characters:

- Bond/M
- Bond/Q
- Bond/Goldfinger
- Bond/Pussy Galore
- Bond/Oddjob

The structural oppositions between Bond and Goldfinger, and Bond and Oddjob, particularly influence the film since confrontations have to be set up between them before the final challenge at the film's resolution. Similarly Bond and Pussy Galore have to have a number of meetings before Bond finally wins her.

ideological functions

There are also structural oppositions between ideologies such as:

- ■ free world/communism
- ■ England/non-English countries
- ■ tradition/modernism

The opposition between modernism and tradition is seen in the sets.

women in goldfinger

Certain characters have obvious and straightforward functions: Q, for instance, represents the mythical wise old man or adviser who gives Bond special weapons to help in his quest; M's role is to represent authority, England and the traditional values that Bond is upholding. At the same time he gives Bond an opportunity to be slightly rebellious.

However, it is the women who have the most significant ideological functions. In order to conform to the beliefs of a patriarchal society the women have to be positioned sexually and politically so that they fulfil the roles expected of them. Miss Moneypenny is not problematic since she is already positioned, being content with her role as secretary and aspiring wife.

There are three other women with whom Bond comes in to contact during his mission: Jill Masterson, Tilly Masterson, and Pussy Galore. All of them are initially 'out of place' either sexually, in that they are initially resistant to Bond, or ideologically in that they are in the service of the villain, or both, like Pussy Galore.

Jill Masterson is in the service of Goldfinger but succumbs easily to Bond's charms, repositioning herself on Bond's side. As a result of this change she is punished by being killed. Her sister Tilly, on the other hand, is an enemy of Goldfinger but is not interested in Bond's charms and because of her independence is murdered. So she is punished, too. Pussy Galore, on the other hand, is in the employ of Goldfinger and initially resistant to Bond's advances. Nevertheless she succumbs and is repositioned both sexually and politically, helping Bond to defeat the villain.

The significance of the repositioning is to indicate that ideologically men are dominant. Even an independent woman like Galore becomes a more subordinate person after repositioning, emphasising the patriarchal view of the inferior place of women in society. Bond's seduction of the heroine serves an ideological purpose in that he 'repositions' her by putting her back into the 'correct' place with the 'correct' views.

Ideologically this keeps women in a subordinate position. When Pussy Galore is trying to get the better of Bond in a fight it is indicative of the growing independence of women, but significantly he wins the fight and the old values triumph. Because of this repositioning of women, the James Bond films can be seen as Oedipal narratives with an Oedipal trajectory.

narration

As well as referring to what Bordwell describes as film forms, narration also refers to information given to us by a character in a film in the form of a voice-over, for example, or in POV shots. Simply, this definition of narration refers to whether we follow the events from the point of view of a particular character, usually the protagonist, or whether the film employs omniscient narration where the audience is given a privileged position and is allowed to see everything.

In *Goldfinger* omniscient narration is employed but since Bond is in almost every scene the audience strongly identifies with him. It is not until Goldfinger assembles the members of the mafia in his rumpus room that Bond is not present although he very quickly arrives to eavesdrop. POV shots are used widely to show events from Bond's perspective. At other times omniscient narration is employed where the audience is given the most appropriate view of a particular scene.

In common with the Oedipal trajectory of the film, Bond's POV shots are explicitly male in which women are objects of what Laura Mulvey terms 'the male gaze'. In other words shots of women in the film are there not necessarily for any narrative purpose but mainly to provide a source of pleasure for the male audience. Other shots of women not from

the male gaze

Bond's POV, for example at Miami, are also what could be termed the male gaze. However, it should be noted that there are also shots where Sean Connery's body is similarly treated, the film makers being aware of his attraction for female members of the audience.

style

introduction

In this section the styles of the films will be examined in relation to how they inform us of narrative and theme. Film style refers to film techniques and with plot it makes up the ingredients of narrative. There are two main areas: editing and mise-en-scène. Mise-en-scène controls what we see in each shot and how we see it, while editing links separate shots and sequences of shots into a coherent order, according to the demands of the film and the director's purpose.

However style also encompasses sound and special effects, both of which are an integral part of the style in *Goldfinger* and other Bond films. John Barry's distinctive musical score is as much a part of the style as the title sequence, as is the dialogue. Also the visual emphasis on technology and gadgetry introduced a stylistic feature without which no Bond movie would be truly 'Bond'. Lastly the dialogue in the film established a tradition of humour and double entendres without which a Bond film would not be the same.

editing

This can control the temporal, spatial, graphic and rhythmic relations between shots. The most common edit in films is the cut which is a simple splice. However edits such as fades and dissolves can indicate the passage of time between the two shots. Space can also be controlled by the juxtaposition of an exterior shot of a house, for example, with an interior of a room, the assumption being that the room is in the house shown previously. Also graphic similarities and differences between shots can be brought to the audience's attention. Finally, the pace of a film can be dictated by the editing, a sequence of rapid cuts injecting excitement into a film and longer gaps between edits giving an air of calm.

The main types of editing are the cut (the simplest, a basic splice of two shots), the fade, where one shot fades to black or goes from black to image, and the dissolve which is the simultaneous fading out of one shot and the fading in of the next so that for a short time both shots are superimposed on screen.

Intercutting is a function of editing which can be very effective in creating suspense. However since Bond is on screen for almost the entire length of the film intercutting is a technique that is really only used during the attack on Fort Knox to create suspense. The film cuts between Bond's struggle inside the vault with Oddjob and the bomb, and the American forces trying to break in.

Peter Hunt's use of editing contributes a great deal to the narrative drive and pace of *Goldfinger*. His links between shots set up connections which help the audience follow events without the need for extraneous dialogue. Also the pace of the film is controlled through the editing. It is normal for films to cut from one shot to another over a continuing action. This is called a match on action.

ACTION SEQUENCE EDITING

In action sequences Hunt utilises a number of techniques to inject excitement. In a match on action he tends to cut just before one would expect, making a fight scene more exciting and other scenes more fast-paced and less pedestrian. By doing so Hunt gives the film a tempo which keeps the audience caught up in the events and therefore unlikely to stop to question any of the numerous inconsistencies in the narrative. Like many editors Hunt utilises short shot lengths in fight scenes and lots of close ups of fists and guns and also fast panning or swish pans. Another way is cutting in the middle of a swish pan which again engenders excitement. This so-called comic strip style was hugely influential on future television action series.

EDITING AND SPECIAL EFFECTS

Clearly many of the special effects in the film, mainly those associated with the Aston Martin, are the result of careful editing. The use of inserts, for

establishing shot

example of real machine gun fire, can give credibility to the effects. (For more about this see Special Effects.)

CONTINUITY EDITING

As previously discussed in Narrative & Form, the film uses continuity editing; the match on action is an example of this. Another feature is the establishing shot when the film cuts to a new sequence and location. For example the sequence in Miami begins with an aerial shot of the hotels, beach and sea to establish not just location but also the appeal of the place; there are similar shots of London – the Thames, Houses of Parliament and Big Ben – and Switzerland's mountains and chalets.

The establishing shot is also used when characters meet before the film cuts to close ups. When Bond meets Goldfinger at the golf club we are given an establishing shot, or two-shot, which places them both in the frame and in the context of their surroundings before cutting to close ups. The first close up is termed shot, and the second reverse, since it is at the reverse end of an imaginary 180 degree line.

mise-en-scène

This refers to features such as setting, costumes, use of black-and-white or colour, set design and special effects, cinematography, and lighting. In *Goldfinger* the mise-en-scène gives the film a glossy, slick look suggesting both high production values and an appealing fantasy world. This was in keeping with the mood of the time; television advertising was beginning to use similar techniques to create a world of consumerism, both attractive and escapist. The mise-en-scène also allows us to compare the modern world of Goldfinger and the traditional world of Bond and the society he is defending. The important features here are setting, set design, use of colour and special effects. Costumes are discussed in Contexts, Representation.

SETTING

One of the ways in which the film presented setting was in the establishing shots mentioned above where the images of the exotic locations seemed to be straight from travel films and brochures, basically stereotypical images associated with these places.

COLOUR

True to the film's theme of gold, the dominant colour in the film is gold and variations of it from yellow to copper. The highly polished surfaces in many of the sets help to give the feeling of gold. In both Goldfinger's Kentucky rumpus room and his Swiss factory, all the surfaces are highly polished and there are wooden floors and shiny brown surfaces elsewhere.

Goldfinger's clothes have a gold theme: he likes to wear a yellow waistcoat and in the golf match he wears a matching cap and cardigan both of which are a yellow check. Other characters in his employ wear gold, notably Pussy Galore. When Bond first meets her she is wearing a gold blouse, at once linking her to Goldfinger. Similarly dressed is Mai Ling, the waitress on Goldfinger's private jet. The death of Jill Masterson by being suffocated when covered with gold paint is another link to Goldfinger. Many objects are gold: Goldfinger's pistol, the canisters of nerve gas, the cushions and the rest of the decor on his private jet. Even his Rolls Royce is predominantly yellow. And of course in Fort Knox there are piles and piles of gold all glittering in the light. Even the table on which Bond is spread eagled and threatened with imminent castration is gold.

However the gold colours are not just linked with Goldfinger but appear elsewhere. The meeting with M, Bond and Colonel Smithers of the Bank of England takes place in a room which exudes wealth and long-established power: the picture frames are gilt, as are the candelabra.

SET DESIGN

Aware that by the time of *Goldfinger* the films functioned as escapist fantasy, any notions of conventional realism were dispensed with. Since naturalism was abandoned the designers had to find a concept which matched the content. The film's visual style is due largely to production designer Ken Adam who saw the films as larger than life and designed sets to match this. The influence of **German Expressionism** is evident, he made the sets reflect a mood rather than reality. The key sets are the inside of the oil tank in the pre-titles sequence, Goldfinger's Swiss factory, his Kentucky rumpus room and the interior of Fort Knox.

In each of these there is an emphasis on large airy interiors. All the surfaces are smooth, consisting of polished metal and glass, with gleaming colours, usually variations of burnished copper or light browns or gold. Even wooden surfaces are highly polished so as to be indistinguishable from the other surfaces. In all, the cinematography emphasises the golden brown tones in the scenes. The sets are modernist in design, minimalist in furnishings and decoration, perfectly fitting the mood of the time and the forward-looking nature of the films. They provide an effective contrast with the more traditional furnishings and sets of the scenes in London.

FORT KNOX

The famous set built by Adam to represent the interior of Fort Knox is pure fantasy, since the weight of gold prevents it being stacked in tall piles as in the film. The film makers were not allowed access to the interior of Fort Knox so Adam had free rein to design the set any way he wanted, with the proviso that he had to design a 'cathedral of gold'. The result was a massive multi-storey set with a lift in the centre and stacks of gold ingots forty feet high behind gleaming chrome bars. The huge ceiling with the central open space and columns on either side is reminiscent of medieval gothic cathedrals and is a perfect setting for the climactic battle at the end.

Other sets such as the rumpus room and Goldfinger's Swiss factory have the same golden brown tones and shining surfaces but reveal the influence of Expressionism in the straight lines and angular beams linking walls and floor.

CINEMATOGRAPHY

It is important not to ignore the impact of Ted Moore's cinematography when discussing the visual impact of the film. It was Moore's responsibility to light the scenes and create the appropriate tones. In Adam's modernist sets Moore chose to use **low key lighting** from a variety of sources in order to enhance the gleaming nature of the surfaces. **High key lighting** would have dissipated the effect.

redolent of taste

Also the camerawork is a vital component of the larger-than-life effect of Adam's sets. Moore tends to use long shots to show the scale of the sets, and how they dominate the human beings in them. Low camera angles are utilised in order to emphasise again the scale, in particular the height and extreme angularity of the ceilings and walls.

Adam's London sets on the other hand, in M's office and the meeting with Colonel Smithers of the Bank of England, emphasise tradition, opulence, and old money whereas the modernist sets emphasise new money. Culture, breeding, elitism, snobbery and even the class system are all present. M's office has wooden panelling but not polished like the modernist sets. Instead it conveys quality of workmanship and opulence, as does the red leather-backed door and the red leather chairs. A wall of books conveys an image of culture and education. The pictures on the wall tend towards the traditional. The room exudes power and traditional values. Miss Moneypenny's office, on the other hand, is very functional, even plain, with little decoration. The difference serves to separate the position of the two people. M is clearly a representative of the traditional values and power structures of England.

This theme is continued in the scene in the Bank of England where Bond, M and Colonel Smithers discuss gold and their suspicions about Goldfinger. At first we see the three of them in a close shot, then the camera tracks back to reveal the huge size of the room in which they are meeting and the enormous table. When the camera pulls back it creates an absurd impression, inviting laughter, but also suggesting power and wealth.

Again like the modernist sets, the room dominates but it is not oppressive, more ridiculous, another part of the humorous nature of the film. The room is redolent of taste and years, if not centuries, of tradition and power. The walls are stone or marble, with arched doorways, suggestive again of a cathedral. In *Goldfinger* gold is worshipped. The walls are covered in gilt-framed paintings of presumably previous governors of the Bank of England, the curtains are gold-coloured, the furniture is antique, there are gold candelabra, and marble ashtrays. A manservant serves cigars which provides a link to Goldfinger and his attempts to train Oddjob as a manservant.

double entendres

Even Bond's Miami hotel room continues the theme with brass fittings and orange-brown walls; before we see Jill lying dead we are aware of a light, off screen, giving the room's furnishings a shimmering look. It is the gold paint which produces this effect.

STYLE AS THEME

One could sum up the contrast between the modernist sets associated with Goldfinger and the more traditional settings in London as the difference between 'old money' and 'new money'. The film could be seen as an attempt by Goldfinger to join the establishment. He has an old Rolls Royce; he has bought an exclusive golf club (perhaps the only way he could join such a place); he tries to train his Korean bodyguard as a manservant with little success. Goldfinger is described as English but does not seem to be. Even his stud farm in the USA seems like an attempt to become accepted, but he is still an obvious outsider. All this seems to indicate xenophobia and even racism on the part of the English Establishment. Goldfinger's attack on Fort Knox could be seen as revenge on the west in general and England in particular since the result would devastate world economies.

dialogue

An important feature of a James Bond film which can be traced back to *Goldfinger* is that the films do not take themselves too seriously; therefore it is expected that the dialogue will contain witty one-liners such as 'Shocking ... positively shocking' delivered after Bond has electrocuted an enemy.

In addition there are the double entendres which are employed again for laughs but also as part of a long tradition of the British cinema, best exemplified by the *Carry On* movies, of sexually suggestive innuendo. When Bond is on the telephone to Felix in the hotel bedroom he looks at the woman on the bed and says he cannot make dinner because 'Something big's just come up'. The innuendo has become a tradition in the films and a source of humour, but is also a way of including sex in the films without being so explicit that the films lose their family rating.

And lastly there are those lines which are an institution and whose appearance in a film is a source of audience pleasure, part of the audience expectation of the genre: 'Bond ... James Bond', and 'Shaken not stirred'.

music

The instantly recognisable James Bond theme with its strident, staccato bass guitar lines was written by Monty Norman but was given an up-tempo arrangement by John Barry. Barry's arrangement reveals influences of both the rock guitar, becoming increasingly prevalent at the time, as well as more traditional brass arrangements, thus being both forward and backward looking, like the film itself. The theme song sung over the opening titles by Shirley Bassey is used to set the scene by being suitably melodramatic as well as informing us of the villain.

FUNCTION OF MUSIC

Firstly music, like all sound in films, can be characterised as **diegetic** or non-diegetic. If diegetic it means that the music comes from within the world of the film, like the music being played in the bodega in the pre-titles sequence of *Goldfinger*. Music which comes from outside the world of the film is non-diegetic. When Bond announces himself to Jill Masterson the accompanying music is non-diegetic.

BONDING

Music can serve to link shots in a sequence and provide continuity. When the attack on Fort Knox takes place the music plays over the entire scene, linking all the shots together.

Music can also provide narrative identification where the spectator is bonded to the narrative by being drawn into the events on screen. In the early days of sound music was felt to be extraneous and was omitted but audiences felt too emotionally distant and so music was restored. Music can also make the audience identify with the characters, as well as identifying particular features of the characters. The use of the James Bond theme at times not only identifies Bond but also indicates certain aspects of his personality, for example he is both dangerous and charismatic.

ANCHORAGE

Music can help reduce the potential number of meanings in a scene. If the music is dramatic, humorous or sad then this will help us interpret the visuals. Music can parallel the visuals by emphasising the intended meaning, or counterpoint the visuals by being in contrast to what is seen, perhaps for a humorous effect or to make an ironical comment.

The James Bond theme is used throughout the film as a motif for Bond himself, as indicated above, and also in certain action scenes. When we first meets Goldfinger in Miami his entrance is accompanied by an arrangement of the theme which is used as a motif to identify him and at other moments of tension and suspense. When Bond introduces himself to Goldfinger in Miami over the radio the Bond theme music plays, injecting a sense of tension into the scene. Similarly we find that the Goldfinger theme is used in many scenes to denote tension, danger and Goldfinger's dominance or domain, for example when the gangsters are trapped in the rumpus room and killed.

Another motif is associated with Oddjob. After he chops down Bond we see a shadow on the wall and a short sharp crescendo of music is played. When Bond next sees Oddjob at the golf club the same music plays instantly providing a connection between the two scenes and identifying Oddjob as the shadowy figure. Here, again, the music serves a very important narrative function.

Throughout the film music is used, usually variations of the two main themes to punctuate and emphasise action sequences or to accentuate the drama of the scene. When Bond is attempting to defuse the nuclear device at Fort Knox the music gets faster and faster and builds in volume as the countdown nears completion, increasing the tension felt by the audience and also conveying the tension felt by Bond.

By and large Barry's music can take two main forms: there is the predominance of insistent brass for action sequences and slush strings are preferred to give a softer feel to the intimate love scenes.

technology and gadgets

The theme song sung by Shirley Bassey was a huge worldwide hit. It began the Bond tradition of having a famous popular singer to sing the title song, which would then enter the pop charts, usually before the film was released, acting as an extra source of publicity.

special effects

One of the most important stylistic features is the prominence of technology and gadgets, symbolic of the futuristic outlook of the film and the series. An important factor is that the technology may seem to be futuristic but only in the near or very near future. In other words it is believable. This includes the gadgets found in the film as well as explosions.

REAR PROJECTION

Surprisingly the film begins with an example of a rather old-established and not very effective special effect: **rear projection**. Location filming in Miami is spliced with close up sequences filmed at Pinewood studios with the Miami footage projected from the rear on to a screen in front of which the actors perform. The problem with rear projection is that the projected scenes have no depth and they are easily distinguishable from the foreground scenes. The reason for this was that Connery was unable to film in Miami and so those scenes were filmed around his absence. In fact Connery did not set foot in the USA at all during filming.

CAR CHASES

In the car chases, particularly through the forest as Bond and Tilly are pursued by Goldfinger's Chinese guards, the camera is under cranked so that when played back at normal speed the motion of the cars is faster. This is surprisingly effective in the film.

ASTON MARTIN DB5

The most famous car in cinema history and an icon of the 1960s, the Aston Martin, was as big an attraction as Sean Connery. It was under-utilised in the film, being used mainly in two short chases and when road rage

special effects style

overtakes Bond. Nevertheless it contributes considerably to the suspense of the film as the audience wait to see its special features being used, particularly the ejector seat. When Bond says 'You're joking' to Q he is only vocalising what the audience is thinking.

Two cars were loaned from Aston Martin who profited greatly from the attendant publicity which, for a time, saw their car as the most desirable in the world. After one of the cars was adapted with the special features it was sold to Eon Productions. Production designer Ken Adam, and special effects supervisor John Stears, adapted one car while the other car was filmed in those scenes where the gadgets were not used.

When the film was released, its huge success forced Aston Martin to build two more replicas which were sent to various events and festivals up until the early 1970s when they were sold off to collectors.

The special features were:

- hydraulic overriders, front and back, which could be used as rams but which were not used in the film
- machine guns hidden behind the front indicator lights
- bullet-proof shield to protect the rear window
- revolving number plates 'valid in all countries'
- high-powered oil jet and nail dispenser (not used for fear of imitation by children) behind rear light clusters
- rear smoke screen
- revolving tyre slasher mounted in hub of nearside rear wheel
- mobile phone hidden in driver's door panel (not seen in film)
- a weapons tray underneath driver's seat (not seen in film)
- radar display screen for tracking vehicles with homing device
- weapons control panel concealed within the centre arm rest
- passenger ejector seat with control button in the top of the gear stick.

The special effects department created the machine guns out of thin metal tubes driven by an electric motor connected to the automobile distributor.

Acetylene gas, as used in a blow torch, was discharged into the tubing to give the effect of gunfire. Shots of actual machine guns were edited in to give more realism.

The tyre shredder was actually a huge screw knife welded to a spare knock-on wheel nut. Unfortunately the car had to stop and the nut be exchanged before the shredder could come out but editing enables it to be seen emerging automatically from the hub centre.

The most famous feature – the ejector seat – was in reality an ejector seat from a fighter plane. However the size of the seat meant that it could only be mounted immediately before the actual shot when a Chinese guard is catapulted through the roof. For the close shots of the interior a normal seat was used.

The popularity of the DB5 caused it to be brought back in *Thunderball*. Undoubtedly much of the suspense of the early part of the film involves the audience wondering when the special features will be used. It has to be said that there is almost a sense of anti-climax when they are, especially as a number of the features are thrown away when Bond indulges in a spot of male chauvinist road rage with Tilly Masterson.

THE LASER

The other memorable technological feature was the industrial laser which is used to threaten Bond's masculinity and later to open the doors of Fort Knox. At the time lasers were rarely seen, and were very much associated with the ray guns of science fiction and not the commonplace technological tool we know today.

However Hamilton discovered that the thin beam of light could not be photographed satisfactorily so an optical effect was employed to create the beam. For the close up of the flame cutting through the gold table top special effects technicians crouched under the table using an oxyacetylene torch to produce the flame making its way through the table and up between Bond's legs. The laser is one of the ways in which the film updates the older genres which influenced the Bond movies. In the old cliffhanger serial a buzzsaw would probably have been used.

NUCLEAR DEVICE

Given the topicality of nuclear weapons, and being only two years after the Cuban Missile Crisis when the USA and the USSR went to the brink of nuclear war, the threatened use of a nuclear device gave the film what was perceived as the main threat of the modern age. In addition China, the 'villain' who supplies the bomb in the film, had recently become a nuclear power and western fears added to the film's topicality.

SEAGULL SNORKEL

One of the early causes of amusement in the film is when a seagull bobbing in the harbour suddenly rises up to reveal that it is really a snorkel device worn by Bond. The laughter from the audience conveys to us that the film makers have a distinctly tongue-in-cheek approach to gadgetry which should not be taken seriously.

contexts

production history

The choice of *Goldfinger* as the third James Bond movie had behind it a marketing strategy to establish Bond as an international phenomenon, particularly in the United States. It was accepted that *Dr No* would establish Bond primarily in Britain, while *From Russia with Love* established Bond as a European success with the exception of France. The third film's US settings and anti-American conspiracy plot were designed to capture the lucrative American market.

Richard Maibaum was again employed to write the screenplay. However, Harry Salzman did not like the first draft so brought in Paul Dehn to rework it. Dehn, who was film critic for the *News Chronicle*, had worked occasionally as a screenwriter and had received a joint Academy award for the Boulting Brothers' *Seven Days to Noon* (1950). Connery was not impressed with the revision so Maibaum was brought in to do the final screenplay.

Terence Young, who had directed the first two Bond movies, began pre-production work on *Goldfinger* but left to direct *The Amorous Adventures of Moll Flanders* (1965). The film was then offered to Guy Hamilton who felt that Bond was far too capable – like Superman there was no suspense as to whether he would deal with any problems sent his way. Hamilton decided to concentrate on the villains, believing that Bond was only as 'good' as his enemies, and Goldfinger and his henchman Oddjob are two of the most memorable Bond villains.

An important point to consider is that there was not a natural progression from *Dr No* to *Goldfinger*. *Goldfinger* is more akin to *Dr No* than the second film, *From Russia with Love*, in terms of the foregrounding of technology and the plot of worldwide conspiracy. With *Goldfinger*, the worldwide conspiracy plot is really established as is the emphasis on technology.

ADAPTATION

Since the film was based on Ian Fleming's novel, it followed the basic storyline but there were problems with adaptation as is always the case when moving from a verbal to a visual medium. One factor which had to be overcome was Fleming's habit of describing sensations and feelings which could not be easily translated into visual images. In addition, adaptation to film has to begin with the realisation that a film has only a limited amount of time in which to tell its story. On the other hand a novel can contain far more information. Therefore adaptations tend to simplify where possible, paring down the original text to its basic ingredients. With *Goldfinger* these are the hero, the violence and sex, the larger than life villain, and the gadgets, although there are relatively few in the novel.

Significant changes include changing Goldfinger's original plan to steal the gold (many critics had mocked this) working out the amount of time and trucks needed to transport such a massive amount. Instead the gold was to be contaminated by radiation from a nuclear device, thus rendering it useless and allowing the Chinese gold to dominate the market. This flaw in the original story is alluded to in the film when Bond makes similar calculations about the problems of the weight of the gold. It was also decided to have a more exciting finale, making it a race against time. Goldfinger, instead of being a member of SMERSH, a Soviet organisation, was backed by Communist China who provides the bomb for him. This was part of a strategy to remove Bond from the context of the Cold War where the traditional enemy was the USSR, and away from the spy thriller. Another factor may have been growing fears in the west about China.

CASTING

As part of a series, casting was straightforward in the regular parts such as M and Miss Moneypenny. Bond was still played by Connery who had been contracted to play the character for four films.

production history

It is worth remembering that other actors were considered for the role of James Bond, including Cary Grant, David Niven, James Stewart and James Mason. However, Connery was eventually chosen after a meeting with Salzman and Broccoli, although what clinched it was when they watched Connery from a window walking across the street. His walk suggested suppleness and toughness, important qualities. It should also be remembered that working on a small budget for the first film meant that a big name star could not be afforded.

That is not to say that Connery was a complete unknown: he had worked in theatre, television and film in a range of roles yet he was undeniably not a major star, but he did see the potential of the role and the fact that it was to be a series. Also, as the leading man he was to be on screen for almost the entire film – a tremendous opportunity. For *Dr No* Connery was paid about $30000, but during *Goldfinger* Connery negotiated a salary increase and five per cent of profits on all Bond films after *From Russia With Love*. This agreement became the subject of a $225 million lawsuit brought by Connery in 1984.

The role of Auric Goldfinger went to German actor Gert Frobe who had been recommended to Guy Hamilton by Broccoli. It was soon apparent that Frobe's lack of English was a serious handicap. Even memorising his lines and parroting them was unsuitable as he tended to say them slowly and clearly. Hamilton told him to say the lines quite fast regardless of intelligibility since that made them easier to dub. The British actor Michael Collins was brought in to dub Frobe's lines.

The part of Goldfinger's henchman Oddjob was played by Harold Sakata, a 284 pound wrestler and former Olympic weight lifter known in his wrestling career as Tosh Togo, which appears on the film's end titles.

With a budget of around three million dollars filming began on 15 January 1964 when Guy Hamilton, cinematographer Ted Moore and production designer Ken Adam flew to Miami to shoot the aerial photography of Miami's Fountainbleau Hotel and other Miami scenery. The only actors involved were Cec Linder who played Felix Leiter, and Austin Willis who played Goldfinger's opponent in the card game. Originally the roles were reversed but their parts were switched at the last minute. Connery

principal photography

was unavailable, as he was completing *Marnie* (1964) with Alfred Hitchcock, which necessitated matching unconvincing rear projection scenes with live action scenes at Pinewood. When Connery arrived at Pinewood principal photography began on 9 March with the pre-titles sequence.

Last minute changes to the script included Q being intolerant of Bond's casual attitude to the special devices his department had created. The bickering between the two of them would subsequently become a staple feature of the series and add more humour. At this point in the script it was decided by Broccoli, against Hamilton's wishes, that it would be more effective for Q to explain about the ejector seat as it would inject suspense as to when it would be used. Broccoli proved to be correct.

After nineteen weeks of principal photography location shooting ended with filming at Andermatt in Switzerland between 7 and 11 July 1964. Second unit photography was done on location in London, Miami Beach, Kentucky and Switzerland and later edited into the scenes shot at and around Pinewood Studios in England. Connery did not go to the United States to film; even Goldfinger's Kentucky stud farm was built on land surrounding Pinewood Studios.

The last scenes filmed were the aerial photography shots of the attack on Fort Knox. The Piper Cubs representing Pussy Galore's Flying Circus buzzed the real Fort Knox, breaking the 5000 feet height restriction in the process by flying over the nearby army base at 500 feet. The soldiers who collapsed supposedly gassed were real soldiers who had been paid $20 and a beer each. As the planes flew overhead they fell down on a cue from the director who blew a whistle from a helicopter hovering nearby.

RELEASE STRATEGY

United Artist and Eon Productions used an unusually large number of prints worldwide – 1100 – so the film could be seen as widely and as quickly as possible. This is a practice now widespread for blockbusters. The purpose is to maximise the effectiveness of the pre-release publicity. The film also benefits this way from word-of-mouth and also reduces the interest payable on the money invested in the film by accelerating the rate

production history

of box-office returns. This approach also creates interest in the film since it turns it into an event.

BONDMANIA

The huge international success of *Goldfinger* led to a phenomenon deemed Bondmania. The success in Britain, accompanied by scenes more reminiscent of pop stars like the Beatles, created a phenomenon duplicated in other countries. After being released in the UK on 17 September 1964, the film was given a major Christmas release in the USA, opening on 22 December 1964 and, unlike the first two films, was premiered in prestigious locations such as Grauman's Chinese Theatre in Hollywood. Queues formed around the block and one cinema in New York showed the film twenty-four hours a day. The worldwide grosses for its first release eventually totalled more than $125 million, an incredible sum in those days, and for a time the film was in the *Guinness Book of Records* as the fastest grossing film in motion picture history.

From Russia With Love established Bond in Europe apart from France which then succumbed like the United States to *Goldfinger*. As well as breaking box office records in Paris the film also broke records around the world, including Tokyo.

Bondmania took James Bond into the wider realms of pop culture more generally to create a cult hero whose popularity was unrivalled in cinema and on a par with the other cultural icons of the decade, the Beatles.

SUCCESS

There are a number of factors involved in the film's success. Firstly Bond films formed a very different entertainment pattern from anything else in popular cinema at the time. Secondly, they succeeded in tapping in to the diverse constituents of an increasingly fragmented audience, appealing to the fantasies of teenagers, young males and females and families.

The image of Britishness represented in Bond was carefully packaged for the international market where the success of British pop culture had created an interest in things British and particularly those things which topical elements

seemed exciting and modern. Bond is a gentleman-hero combined with the toughness and sexual magnetism of the Hollywood leading men, a perfect role-model for the hedonistic 1960s. Lastly, the exotic foreign locations are presented with all the glossy sophistication of an upmarket travel brochure, making the cosmopolitan nature of the films' locations part of their appeal. *Goldfinger* won an Academy Award for Norman Wanstall's sound effects.

In the 1960s the films seemed modern and new whereas now they are an institution. However, they still manage to retain their appeal through careful updating of the formula and keeping topical elements in the films. In addition, changing the actor playing Bond from time to time keeps him forever ageless, or at least thirty-five.

social context

The cinematic Bond was a product of the changing social and cultural conditions of the 1950s and 1960s. Britain had changed throughout the 1950s from a post-war society still suffering under the deprivations of rationing in the early 1950s to a society increasingly prosperous and becoming more consumer-oriented. By 1959 the Conservative government under Harold MacMillan could proudly announce to the public, 'You've never had it so good'. The prosperity being experienced by the British public continued into the 1960s. On a world scale the election of President Kennedy in the USA seemed to signal great faith in the future and in youth in particular. In Britain the election of a Labour Government under Prime Minister Harold Wilson was trumpeted as a break with the past. Wilson's government was presented as 'new' – modern and meritocratic rather than old-fashioned and class-bound.

The cinematic James Bond in the form of Sean Connery exemplified this 'cultural revolution' where prominence was given to science, technology and technological progress. From *Goldfinger* onwards the Bond films contributed to this obsession with new technology by foregrounding it and fetishing it and the gadgets were often authentic, e.g. the laser. An examination of the Bond films from *Dr No* onwards reveals that not only do the films use the latest developments or technology a few years in

social context

advance of reality, they also take advantage of topical developments in the plots. For example in *Dr No* the plot about missile launches being sabotaged mirrors problems with real US launch problems.

This topicality and emphasis on technological development perfectly reflected the 1960s and was a huge factor in establishing the popularity of the series. It was, however, not the only factor: attitudes to sex and consumerism also played a part, as well as the fact that the films, such as *Goldfinger*, could be backward-looking as well as forward-looking.

Not only was there a shift to consumerism and prosperity in the late 1950s and 1960s, which is mirrored perfectly in the films, there was also a shift in morals and attitudes to sexuality. Although the 1960s are often characterised as the decade of permissiveness, the change began in the 1950s. Sex became increasingly less of a taboo subject and was treated more frankly in the press, theatre, novels and advertising, although this treatment was still tame by today's standards.

By the 1960s the notion of the 'permissive society' had appeared, epitomised by the obscenity trial of *Lady Chatterly's Lover* by D.H. Lawrence. By the time of the release of *Goldfinger* the term 'Swinging London' had entered the vocabulary. Swinging London represented a more hedonistic, liberated, permissive Britain. The most significant factor was the emergence of a genuinely indigenous form of pop music spearheaded by the Beatles. Suddenly youth seemed to be in control: music, clothes, attitudes all changed. The sexual permissiveness was epitomised in the new fashions, particularly the mini-skirts and designs of Mary Quant.

James Bond was the perfect hero for the permissive society: he was hedonistic, sexually active, progressing from one girl to another and treating them with the same casual indifference he shows to Q's gadgets.

In British cinema a new generation of attractive and sexy stars with international appeal had arisen, for example Julie Christie, Terence Stamp and Michael Caine. Not only did these actors play characters who were hedonistic and liberated but many of them used regional accents, no longer conforming to the class-conscious image of British leading men and ladies which had lasted well into the 1950s.

British film industry

Thus in politics, fashion, music and other aspects of popular culture the 1960s represented a break with the past and a celebration of all that was new and different. The Bond films were just one component of a new British popular culture which emphasised youth, sex appeal and modernity.

industrial context

Another factor in the enormous success of the early films such as *Goldfinger* was the British film industry. The 1950s was not considered to be a classic decade for British films. Favourite genres were the war film, the crime thriller and comedy. The films were criticised for being backward-looking and conforming to an image of Britain which, if it had not already disappeared, was at least changing radically. Leading actors tended to portray middle class characters who spoke with cut-glass accents. Regional accents were reserved for certain comedies or comic relief in other films.

By the end of the 1950s, however, there were changes taking place. First of all there was the huge success in Britain, and internationally, of the Hammer horror films, beginning with *The Curse of Frankenstein* (1957), and *Dracula* (1958). Hammer's lurid horror movies with their emphasis on gore, bright colours and sexuality attracted a youthful audience to the cinema through their blend of sex, violence and anti-heroes. Although very successful they were still costume dramas and therefore could be considered backward looking. Nevertheless they are important for being instrumental in helping to create a more liberal, if titillating attitude to sex.

The other trend in British cinema in the late 1950s and early 1960s was the New Wave films which emphasised social relevance and realism over the escapism of Hammer. Less commercially successful but critically acclaimed, these films produced a whole host of new stars, tended to be shot in black and white and were more frank in their treatment of sex and class divisions. These films often concerned themselves with the English regions and working class life which had rarely before been depicted in such a serious manner. Natural lighting and real locations were preferred.

These films had lost their popularity by 1963, however. Lindsay Anderson's *This Sporting Life* (1963), generally thought to be the last of the New

Wave films, was a commercial and critical failure and by this time the British public had grown tired of them. The optimism of the 1960s was not present in these films and that is probably one factor in their decline.

By this time British audiences wanted films which reflected optimism, films which celebrated the new world in which they lived. The Bond films were perfectly placed to take advantage of this change. Their preposterous plots, exotic foreign locations and glossy visuals created a fantasy world which had more relevance to the consumer-oriented, technologically-obsessed society around them than the kitchen-sink dramas of the New Wave.

The fact that the British public was looking for something new, to reflect the changing society in which they now lived, was also indicated by the fact that there were other non-realist genres emerging in the 1960s. These included pop musicals and films which took advantage of 'Swinging London'.

The Bond films reflected the social changes taking place in the 1960s as well as changes in the British film industry. But there is another factor in the appeal of the films which *is* backward-looking. Throughout the 1950s Britain found itself having to come to terms with being a lesser power. The Empire was being granted independence, Britain had failed to assert itself over the Suez debacle and there was a general feeling that, in world politics, Britain was not the major player it had been. A major part of the success of the films is the way they combine the futuristic elements, embodied in the technology and Bond's attitude to sex, with a successful portrayal of Britain as at least the equal of the USA and still a major world player.

genre

All genres are not immutable but change over the years or go out of fashion. Genre has four functions:

- industrial
- audience

repetition

■ mythic
■ ideological

For the film industry genre films take some of the risk out of film making by repeating previously successful formulas in the hope that the success will be repeated. For audiences they also remove risk by giving an indication of what to expect and by allowing audiences to gain extra pleasure from the chance to demonstrate their generic competencies. Genre films also have a mythic function, providing simple solutions to problems, as well as an ideological function, reinforcing existing dominant attitudes and beliefs, due to the essentially conservative nature of genre.

Essentially genre involves the repetition of a set of features from setting, character, plots, to conventions and structures. However, problems can set in with a genre like horror which has many sub-genres and whose visual features, such as setting, can alter drastically. Different genres are often merged in one film. What is *The Rocky Horror Picture Show* (1975) – a horror film or a musical? To answer this question one should take Rick Altman's advice and examine the syntax or structure of the film, as opposed to the semantics which refer to the visuals and sound elements of the film. So a film like *The Rocky Horror Picture Show* belongs more properly to the musical since it is structured around the need to have songs and dances.

A film like *Star Wars*, however, has borrowed its syntax from the western but it would be misleading to think of it as a western since the semantics in this case take precedence with the audience. Also, narrative resolutions are often specific to particular genres: the musical likes to finish with a big set-piece song-and-dance number while westerns have a shootout either between individuals or else between opposing groups such as the US cavalry and bands of Red Indians.

On its own *Goldfinger* would not be a genre film but when a number of Bond films are examined then common features emerge. While *Goldfinger* follows the pattern set by *Dr No* it is the film which really establishes the Bond films as a genre in its own right, introducing essential ingredients specific to the James Bond genre

such as a tongue-in-cheek approach to violence, the double entendres, and the emphasis on technology.

A useful exercise is to split the film into components which can be found in any film and look for similarities. These features are:

- narrative structure
- settings
- costumes/props
- characters
- plots
- situations
- conventions

As discussed above the visual indicators may not be sufficient to indicate genre, a better guide being the film's narrative structure and resolution. Certainly with Bond the gun barrel sequence, the pre-titles, the resolution where Bond first defeats the villain's plans then is intimate with the girl as a reward, are all specific to the James Bond genre, even although the basic structure can be found elsewhere, in action thrillers and other genres.

When we examine *Goldfinger* in relation to other Bond films, both before and more particularly after, we find that the film fits all the criteria.

SETTINGS

Goldfinger utilises international locations, in particular those considered exotic and appealing, and they are often filmed as if from a travelogue. The locations were particularly important at a time when international holiday travel was beginning to become more widespread. The other setting is Britain, usually London. Here the depiction is very traditional (see Representation) but is designed to present Britain in a very appealing manner to audiences outside the country.

COSTUMES

The Bond films are not costume dramas, being set in contemporary times, but there are a couple of consistent features regarding costume. Bond will always be dressed formally, with expensively tailored suits, while women will be scantily dressed at times. In *Goldfinger*, there are shots of women in bikinis and, later, tight catsuits for Pussy Galore's circus.

PROPS

Obviously the props in *Goldfinger*, and subsequent films, centre around the technological gadgetry such as the Aston Martin DB5 with all its inbuilt devices, the homing devices, and Goldfinger's laser. But more bizarre items, such as Oddjob's steel rimmed bowler hat which he uses, frisbee-style, to kill people are also included.

CHARACTERS

Goldfinger contains a number of characters who would become regular features in later films. First of all there is the villain, Auric Goldfinger. Like all villains he should be memorable and a worthy adversary. Although English he appears to be foreign, as are most of the villains to be found in the films. He is a larger-than-life character, rich, with what amounts to a private army and bases all over the world. He has a henchman, Oddjob, who is also a typically exotic villain with skills which are difficult to defeat, in this case, martial arts and a lethal bowler hat.

Other characters are the women, or girls as they are usually referred to, and include those in minor roles whose purpose is to decorate the screen and act as an attraction for Bond. They function basically to show how attractive Bond is. Other women characters include helpless sympathetic women who may need to be rescued. *Goldfinger* contains two women who are in this category, although both ultimately are killed for siding with Bond, Jill Masterson and her sister, Tilly. But there are also women who are dangerous and on the opposing side until repositioned by Bond, in this case Pussy Galore. The name is another feature of the characters in a Bond film: they should have exotic names, often suggestive. One of these women always represents Bond's reward at the end of the film. Another female character is Miss Moneypenny, M's secretary who represents a more traditional sort of woman, and is part of the regular cast.

Other regular members of the cast include Bond's boss, M, and Q who provides Bond with his equipment.

Last of all is the character of Bond. Certain features remain constant: his sophistication, womanising, humour and sadism. Although the actor may change, it can be argued that Sean Connery created the template for future Bonds who have, by and large and allowing for social changes, stuck to the stereotype created.

PLOTS

From Russia With Love, the second film, with its plot to discredit Bond, was an aberration. As in Goldfinger plots usually involve some attempt at world domination. From Goldfinger onwards international conspiracy organisations such as SPECTRE, or megalomaniacs such as Goldfinger replaced the usual threat from the Soviet Union. The series as it progressed followed world events, with the British Secret Service and James Bond joining forces with the Russians against a common enemy. This fine-tuning of the plots to take account of political changes is another reason why the films have continued to be successful.

SITUATIONS

No Bond film would be complete without a variety of set piece situations. Like many modern blockbusters one could argue that Goldfinger, and other Bond films, are constructed around a series of situations which are more important than the plot. Among these would be the confrontation at the film's climax. This involves defeating the villain in a setting suitably memorable and dramatic, such as Fort Knox. These unusual and dramatic locations are a standard of the Bond films. Other situations involve Bond being placed in a life-threatening position such as being strapped to a table with a laser bean moving up between his legs.

Again, the success of Goldfinger encouraged the producers to make this a staple of the genre. Interestingly Goldfinger's set piece situations are rarely to do with violence: the death of Jill Masterson, covered in gold paint, is the aftermath of unseen violence; the golf match is tense and an integral part of the plot but completely without any action.

distinctive formula

CONVENTIONS

Among the many conventions in Bond films which we find in *Goldfinger* is the method of death employed. There have to be a number of bizarre deaths: Jill Masterson is suffocated by being covered in gold paint; her sister Tilly has her neck broken by Oddjob's steel-rimmed bowler; the gangster Mr Solo is part of a car which is reduced to a small cube of metal in a car crusher; and Goldfinger himself is sucked out of an aeroplane window.

product differentiation

Films, like other commercial products, need to differentiate themselves from other films in order to try to succeed. Each genre's features separate them from others. Within the action thriller genre, which the Bond movies are related to, the way in which they are differentiated from the Hollywood product is through their Britishness. All the American action thrillers tend to have blue-collar heroes such as Bruce Willis in the *Die Hard* movies, or Sylvester Stallone or Arnold Schwarzenegger. There is no sophisticated or British counterpart to Bond with his links back to earlier British heroes.

PRODUCTION IDEOLOGY

What became the Bond genre through repetition and variation was described by Broccoli as its Production Ideology which was based on the notion of what is or is not 'Bondian'. This constitutes a set of expectations about what a Bond film should be like, what it should contain, how it should be made, and its style. The term 'Bondian' essentially means 'in the spirit of James Bond' and has become a term used to describe a distinctive formula.

If genre films repeat and vary formula – the stories, characters and situations are all familiar to the audience but are sufficiently different from previous films as to prevent the audience becoming bored – then the Bond films certainly qualify as a genre of their own.

The variations needed to sustain genre are part of Bond's success – different exotic locations, gadgets, villains, but similar situations in similar plots, even a different James Bond from time to time. These variations have enabled the films to adapt to changing ideological and cultural conditions.

The Bond films are genre films since there is a basic formula which stays remarkably consistent throughout the series. The familiarity of the audience with stories, character types and narrative situations of the films gives rise to expectations regarding their recurrence in each new film.

OTHER INFLUENCES

However, James Bond owes a debt to previous types of genres. James Chapman (Chapman, 2000) identifies two which have had an influence, both of which have, like Bond, their antecedents in literature.

IMPERIALIST SPY THRILLER

It can be argued that the James Bond films are the end of a line of what Chapman terms the British Imperialist Spy Thriller. The antecedents are primarily literary – Fleming's novels have links with John Buchan's novels featuring Richard Hannay and 'Sapper's' (H.C. McNeile) hero Bulldog Drummond. These heroes tend to be upper-class, privately educated, xenophobic and completely loyal to king, country and empire. Like them, Bond is patriotic, honest, and an upright defender of the nation with adjustments in character to fit contemporary morals.

Closest to Bond is probably Bulldog Drummond, particularly when played by Ronald Colman who combined toughness and cynicism with sophistication. Another popular film hero who had an influence on Bond was Simon Templar, alias the Saint, who was revitalised in the 1960s with the television series starring Roger Moore. He later succeeded to the role of James Bond on the strength of his success as the Saint.

The nearest equivalent to James Bond could be said to be the subject of a popular British radio series – Dick Barton. Barton repeated his radio success when transferred to cinema in the late 1940s by Hammer Films who made three low-budget movies. Like Bond, Barton was to be found confronting sinister super-criminals and masterminds whose conspiracies threatened Britain. There are a number of comparisons to Bond: he had special agent status; the plots involved chases and action sequences; and he had his own very distinctive theme tune, 'The Devil's Gallop'. This piece of music, like John Barry's arrangement of the James Bond theme, perfectly captured the pace and excitement of the events.

The genre described above tended to consist of low budget films rather than 'A' class films. The significance of the James Bond films to the film industry is that they upgraded a traditional low budget genre to one with high production values: an 'A' class genre.

CLIFFHANGER ADVENTURE THRILLER

The other cinematic genre which Chapman identifies as an antecedent to James Bond is the cliffhanger adventure serial. If any cinematic genre inherited the mantle of the Saturday matinee serials and Pearl White tied to the rails it was James Bond.

The film serial or 'chapter play' evolved in the silent era, encompassing the exploits of Pearl White who, literally, could be found hanging from cliffs, through to the serials of Flash Gordon and Buck Rogers, and even Batman. This form of film making can be seen as an alternative to the dominant classical cinema of Hollywood. It represented the continued existence of a cinema based on 'attractions' (stunts, chases, fights, death-defying escapes) and on the non-closure of narrative (at least until the final chapter) – 'Bond will return' indicates the continuing unending nature of the series. Like these serials Bond films tend to be constructed around set pieces involving stunts or special effects or Bond in a dangerous life-threatening situation.

While the serials ranged across various genres, including westerns, adventure melodramas, science-fiction and crime-fighter serials, in the collective consciousness of cinemagoers they have come to represent a cinema of thrills, spills, master-criminals and imperilled heroines.

The difference with them and Bond is that the Bond films are bigger and more expensive. The master criminals were better characterised and more threatening to introduce more suspense about the final outcome, and the inventions are more believable – a major strength of the Bond movies is that the technology is only slightly futuristic and certainly believable.

British film industry

To the traditional elements of suspense and the traditional characters was added sex in the form of sexy girls often scantily clad. The sex was hinted at rather than being explicit so as not to lose the family audience. Instead of a week-to-week continuation, the Bond films are self-contained but each film ends with the announcement that Bond will return. Also the pre-titles sequence often has Bond finishing off a previous mission as in *Goldfinger*, again emphasising the continuing nature of the films.

institutions

UNITED ARTISTS

This was founded in 1919 by four stars of the silent screen: Charlie Chaplin, Douglas Fairbanks, Mary Pickford, and director D.W. Griffith. They felt that they would have more control over their pictures and therefore make more money if they distributed them independently. However, by the time sound arrived in 1926 the company had serious financial problems. Nevertheless the arrival of television in the late 1940s and early 1950s gave the studio an advantage over those production companies which still maintained their own studios. As television caused the market for films to contract, and the major studios had to sell off their assets, United Artists attracted film makers who could make films without the overheads of the other studios.

By the early 1960s United Artists had contributed to the revival of the British film industry by backing films such as *Tom Jones* (1963) which won four Oscars, *The Knack* (1965) which won the Palm d'Or, the first Beatles movie, *A Hard Day's Night* (1964), as well as the James Bond films. At a time when the old studio system had collapsed United Artists showed the way forward. This company also financed American films which would be very influential in the revitalisation of Hollywood in the 1960s – *Easy Rider* (1969), *The Graduate* (1967), and *Bonnie and Clyde* (1967). When United Artists found itself in financial troubles again in the late 1970s it was the Bond movies which kept it afloat. Having been bought over by Transamerica, a San Francisco-based insurance group, the company was later sold to MGM after the financial disaster of *Heaven's Gate* (1980).

merchandising potential

The importance of UA was that it showed the way of the future, after the collapse of the studio system, and became a template for independent film production. The decline and fragmentation of the audience had important consequences for the film industry. There was now a tendency to concentrate on fewer but bigger budget films intended to reap individual profits: the origins of the 'blockbuster'. After *Dr No* all Bond films were treated as such.

EON PRODUCTIONS

This film production company was formed by Harry Salzman and Albert R. Broccoli. The name is an acronym which stands for 'Everything or nothing'. Salzman sold off his interest to United Artists in 1975. Eon is a subsidiary of Danjaq SA, a European company named after Dana and Jacqueline, the wives of Broccoli and Salzman respectively.

marketing

Goldfinger can be credited with being the first film to fully exploit its merchandising potential. While the film was aggressively marketed to maximise audience interest, it is in the way the film became the focus of merchandising agreements, and even product placement, that made the film so influential on the development of commercial cinema.

MARKETING

Sean Connery had lost enthusiasm for the part of Bond when the film's release was due and was reluctant to submit himself to the questions of reporters. Other cast members were given responsibility to publicise the film, in particular Honor Blackman. For publicity tours she was given an actual gold finger to wear which necessitated security guards accompanying her everywhere. Shirley Eaton, too, undertook international publicity tours to highlight her role as the 'golden girl'. The famous Aston Martin DB5 was also used in publicity campaigns around the world including the 1964 World Fair.

It was with *Goldfinger* that *Playboy* began the practice of photographing the Bond starlets, a practice which became a tradition. Shirley Eaton, the 'golden girl' who was covered in gold paint in the film appeared on the cover of *Life* in September 1964. Both the theme song sung by Shirley Bassey and the soundtrack album by John Barry became major hits. The song reached number eight in the top ten chart in the USA, and the soundtrack album went gold.

SPIN OFFS

Goldfinger arguably paved the way for the modern phenomenon of multi-media marketing and utilising the film's fame in a range of products. The most famous example of this was Corgi Toys' model of the DB5 which became the best-selling toy of the year. The licensing agreement between Corgi and Eon became the longest agreement in cinema history with Corgi continuing to produce the car to this day.

Long after the première, products were still being produced to cash in on the film's popularity. These included jigsaw puzzles, board games, an action doll of Oddjob, which actually threw the bowler hat, and a set of bubble gum cards which caused a scandal due to the proliferation of scantily clad women in them and were eventually withdrawn (but not before this author had collected almost all of them).

Galeries Lafayette in Paris opened a 'James Bond Boutique' selling 007 cufflinks and shirts. An Australian lingerie manufacturer created a range of women's underwear with the selling slogan 'Become fit for James Bond'.

Sales of the original novels, as tie-ins with the films, with images from the films on the covers peaked in the mid-1960s.

By the time of *Thunderball*'s release the producers had realised the value of spin-off products and the 007 gun logo could be found on a wide range of products including shoes, raincoats, aftershave and underwear.

When one examines the blockbusters of today, designed to take advantage of the multi-media potential of the parent companies, with toys, games and soundtrack albums all being produced, the influence of *Goldfinger* and the rest of the Bond films is obvious. Even today Bond is in the forefront of film merchandising. *The World is Not Enough* had agreements to license

Representation in films

merchandise including toy guns, trading cards, model cars, walkie-talkies, personal organisers, clothing, playing cards, radios, razors, posters, CDs and documentary videos.

PRODUCT PLACEMENT

The positioning of particular goods in the film, in return for a fee or free use of the product, is widespread now and while it does seem a relatively new phenomenon, its origins can be traced back to *Goldfinger*. There are relatively few products seen or mentioned by name in the film although the most famous and the most obvious one is Bond's car, the Aston Martin DB5. There are other examples: when Felix Leiter is shadowing Bond at the Kentucky stud he is photographed with a Kentucky Fried Chicken outlet behind him. It was also rumoured that Harry Salzman had done a deal with Gillette to use their shaving products when Bond is shaving on Goldfinger's private jet, although it is impossible to see the name on the product.

Again, by the time of *The World is Not Enough* the product placement was far more organised; agreements existed with BMW, Omega, Heineken, Samsonite, Calvin Klein, John Smith's Extra Bitter, Microsoft and Hershey's.

ideology

This is a term familiar to us from political parties but the concept is much wider than that, describing a set of interlocking ideas, values and beliefs which can be held by individuals or groups within society. Ideology is often presented as 'natural' or 'self-evident' so that the beliefs are rarely questioned but taken for granted. Ideology which is defined as representing an entire society or country actually emanates from particular social groups whose influence over affairs is greatest – 'the ruling classes'. The dissemination of their ideological beliefs as 'common sense' naturalises these beliefs, and enables the elite groups to continue to run the country.

This dominant ideology is disseminated through institutions such as the education system, the political system, and the mass media, including cinema. Representation in films is controlled by ideology since the attitudes of those creating the representations will be reflected in the way a country, social group or individual is represented.

The criticism of *Goldfinger* by the communist *Daily Worker* indicates what the dominant ideology of the film is: Bond represents the free world against the communist world represented by China. The plot involves disrupting the capitalist system by rendering useless the gold reserves of the USA and allowing China to benefit. This reflected growing fears of China at the time. In addition the gold reserves of Fort Knox are an ideal symbol of the west and capitalism. Ideologically the film also foregrounds the elitist nature of British society: even although Bond himself, with Connery's Scottish accent, is less obviously a product of the class system the same cannot be said for the other members of the establishment who appear in the film: M, and Colonel Smithers, for example. Remarks are made about defending Queen and country and thus the British way of life and its traditions.

Bond does seem faintly rebellious when confronted by M, and later the Bankers, so this may be a nod to the fact that within society the class system was beginning to break down. Bond is representative of the traditional ruling elite while also in his minor rebellions, reflecting the changes within society.

Ideologically the film also exhibits a certain xenophobia: the enemy behind Goldfinger is Chinese, his henchman is Korean, and Goldfinger himself although English seems to be more German. He is an outsider who tries to become part of the British Establishment – he owns an exclusive golf course, for example – and dresses his henchman Oddjob in the clothes of an English butler again emphasising his desire to be accepted. The absurdity of Oddjob in the clothes only emphasises how ridiculous it is for foreigners to be part of the English Establishment, and further enhances the xenophobia of the film.

Although in many ways the film is forward-looking, ideologically it still places Britain in a greater role in world affairs than in reality, particularly concerning the relationship with the United States. The CIA operative Felix Leiter is less an equal than an assistant to Bond, even when Bond is operating in the USA.

class element

Another feature of the film's ideology is its patriarchy. Bond is part of a male-dominated society where men are active, dominant and capable, while women are generally submissive, helpless and give in sooner or later to Bond's charms. In *Goldfinger* any women who do not fit this pattern are punished by being killed, like Tilly, or are repositioned by Bond, like Pussy Galore.

representation

JAMES BOND

The Britishness of Bond differentiates him from American action heroes and was carefully packaged for the international market. The traditional toughness and sexual charisma of Hollywood leading men is combined with more English qualities: Bond is a gentleman (although his dealings with women may make this a loose term) who can appear snobbish about the good things of life: clothes, fine wine and brandy, for example. Therefore there are scenes where he is seen showing his knowledge of expensive drinks, and he is almost always dressed in expensively-tailored suits and black ties (the blue towelling beach suit in Miami is an obvious aberration).

The class element of Bond found in the novels is missing thanks to Sean Connery's Scottish accent which removes him from the English class system, but still marks him out as British for foreign audiences. In fact one should not underestimate the influence of Connery in conveying the image of Bond found in the film. Bond is also clearly a male chauvinist when it comes to women. The phrase 'love them and leave them' comes to mind, and his attitude is summed up by his slap on the bottom of the masseuse, Dink, in Miami.

WOMEN

Given the patriarchal nature of society in which the film was made, and the fact that women were only just beginning to assert themselves and the women's liberation movement was in its very early beginnings, it is not surprising that the images of women in the film tend to show them as sex objects or women whose only ambition is to settle down with a suitable man. Miss Moneypenny is the prime example of this, flirting with Bond who indulges her but who we assume is too staid and boring for Bond. This is emphasised by her pearls and twinset, the epitome of a conservative, traditional woman.

Dink, with her bathing suit, blonde hair, and vaguely squeaky voice is the archetypal bimbo who exists simply as a means of sexual gratification for the hero. Jill Masterson is first seen in black underwear, a code at the time for less than pure morals, so it is no surprise that she sleeps with Bond.

PUSSY GALORE

Pussy is a thinly disguised lesbian, represented as 'butch' in terms of her man's clothes, judo and the phrase, 'I'm immune', which she says as a rebuff to Bond's charms. Although women were beginning to assert themselves politically and sexually, the film is more reflective of traditional views, and treats lesbianism rather coyly even though the homosexual debate had begun a few years earlier. Perhaps there was a nod to the family audiences the films were aimed at.

The representation of women in *Goldfinger* is indicative of the ideological processes at work in cinema. As in other popular 1960s films there are relatively few women on screen with sizable speaking parts. However, there are a number of narrative traits to be found: their actions are motivated by self-interest – like Jill Masterson who works for Goldfinger simply because he pays her and not out of loyalty, and is easily persuaded to change sides by Bond, showing another trait, and that they are highly susceptible to male influence. Even Pussy Galore, a lesbian (overt in the novel but less obviously so in the film) succumbs rather easily to Bond's charms once he establishes his male superiority in their fight in the barn.

This demonstrates another trait; women tend to be incompetent in at least one skill crucial to the narrative: Tilly Masterson's incompetence with a gun results in her death and Bond's capture; Pussy Galore's judo skills are no match for Bond, and although she is a competent pilot when Goldfinger's private jet is out of control it is Bond who remains calm.

expectations

All in all, the function of women in the film is to highlight the natural superiority of the male in the form of Bond and to act as a reward for the successful completion of his mission. Although attitudes to women have changed since 1964, and this is reflected in later Bond films, by and large even the independent, more assertive women succumb to Bond in the end.

censorship

Goldfinger was released at a time when censorship laws were being relaxed in literature and the theatre, and even in films there was a more adult approach to matters such as homosexuality as in films such as Joseph Losey's *The Servant* (1963). However graphic depictions of sex of any kind were still many years away and this was reflected in *Goldfinger*. Traditionally when Bond seduces a girl the camera cuts away just as things get interesting and there is no nudity. Although the depiction of sex and nudity has relaxed over the years, the Bond films still adhere to the depiction of sex established in the early films. Anything else would threaten the families and young teenagers who are a major and very important part of the overall audience.

The name of Pussy Galore greatly concerned United Artists who thought that its sexual connotations were too strong and urged, without success, that the name be changed to Kitty Galore.

audience

As stated earlier, audiences help construct genres through their expectations. There are two ways of looking at audiences: that they are passive – they receive information from the text on the screen in a one-way process, without contributing anything themselves. The other more prevalent view is that audiences are active. In other words rather than meaning simply being given to them they actively construct meaning through their own set of competences which include age, sex, social and cultural backgrounds, and also their preexisting generic and filmic knowledge. Therefore, instead of an audience being considered as one

filmography

mass which interprets films in the same way, audiences are now seen as individuals who construct individual meanings according to the factors above. This is not to say that each person will interpret a film differently but that the potential to do so is there.

Originally film audiences were seen as one mass to be attracted but within the last twenty to thirty years film audiences have become increasingly fragmented. Instead of aiming at a mass audience specifically, film studios aim at niche audiences. Of course mass audiences are important, and the bigger the movie's budget the more likely the appeal to a mass audience. However, rather than seeing this audience as one amorphous group, it is split up into smaller groups. *Goldfinger* followed a trend begun in the late 1950s of spending more money on fewer films in order to attract audiences with what was seen as an event movie.

For any James Bond film, the expectations of the audience are paramount; thus after *Goldfinger* the genre was basically stabilised with the features that found popularity with audiences, and the composition of the target audience was kept to the fore. Thus in more liberal times Bond films are still coy about sex and do not show violence which is too explicit.

filmography

In any study of *Goldfinger* it is worthwhile examining other films. First of all *Dr No* and *From Russia With Love*, both directed by Terence Young, indicate the basic outline of the genre in the former while the latter shows the direction that Bond did not take. It was chosen as the second film because it was President Kennedy's favourite novel. *Thunderball*, also directed by Terence Young, demonstrates great similarities to *Goldfinger* but utilises the successful features more deliberately to produce one of the most celebrated films of the 1960s. Although the films had different directors their similarities demonstrate the importance of the formula over any authorial style.

The James Bond films spawned many imitators particularly in the wake of the unprecedented success of *Goldfinger*. These imitators included the *Matt Helm* series starring Dean Martin, another American series staring

deliberate spoof

James Coburn, of which the first, *Our Man Flint* (1965), was the best. These imitations tended to exaggerate and emphasise the distinct qualities of Bond. The television series *The Man from UNCLE* and its film spin offs were also closely modelled on Bond, with the agents, world conspiracies and global terrorist organisation THRUSH, a thinly disguised SPECTRE.

Some films brought out in the wake of *Goldfinger* tried to depict a more accurate image of spies and secret agents. *The Ipcress File* (1964), directed by Sidney J. Furey from the novel by Len Deighton, starred Michael Caine as Harry Palmer. The film was produced by Harry Salzman and had a soundtrack composed by John Barry. An attempt to marry the espionage thriller with the social realism of the New Wave, it is an interesting film to compare to *Goldfinger* given its connections through personnel.

Another film which attempted to portray a more realistic image of the secret agent is Sidney Lumet's *The Spy Who Came in from the Cold* (1965) from the novel by John le Carré. Again there were associations with Bond through Paul Dehn who co-scripted the film.

Perhaps the most blatant attempt to cash in on the success of Bond and Connery in particular was the Italian film *Operation Kid Brother* (1968) which starred Neil Connery, Sean's brother, and familiar faces from previous Bond films. It was a commercial and critical disaster, a blatant attempt at exploitation.

An examination of contemporary thrillers, such as Bruce Willis' *Die Hard* movies, will reveal similarities with Bond. However James Cameron's *True Lies* (1994) starring Arnold Schwarzenegger, has many of the features of a Bond movie with Schwarzenegger as a kind of super-Bond, and could be said to pay homage to the Bond genre.

Lastly Mike Myers' film *Austin Powers: International Man of Mystery* (1997) is a deliberate spoof of the James Bond genre and as well as being very funny is very accurate in the features of the genre it is lampooning.

critical responses

Goldfinger was, by and large, well received by the public and press alike. *Kinematograph Weekly* announced:

critical responses

> The incredible, almost impossible plot is carried along from one smashing incident to another and the ability of the more astonishing incidents to provoke admiring laughter as well as chills is a tribute to screenwriting, direction and stars.

The *Monthly Film Bulletin* was similarly full in its praise:

> *Goldfinger* really is a dazzling object lesson in the principle that nothing succeeds like excess.

There were dissenting voices, notably the *Daily Worker*, a newspaper run and controlled by the Communist Party of Great Britain whose critic, Nina Hibben, reviewed it not as simple entertainment but as an ideological vehicle and tool of capitalism:

> *Goldfinger* is one vast confidence trick to blind the masses to what is going on underneath.

More interestingly Penelope Houston, editor of *Sight and Sound*, the leading intellectual film journal of the time, reflected the way the serious critics had now tried to come to terms with the success of the Bond films and no longer dismissed them as forgettable escapist entertainment. The huge success of *Goldfinger* and the penetration of Bond into many aspects of popular culture meant that critics tried to take them seriously. Houston compared them to elements of the French *Nouvelle Vague* and attributed the success of *Goldfinger* and the other Bond films to catching the mood of the times, but thought this would not last:

> In a few years the films will seem dated by their assumptions as much as by the lines of their cars, or by Pussy Galore's extravagant leathery wardrobe: the screen's Bond is at once the last of the clubland buccaneers and the first of the joke supermen. The transformation has earned the film makers their place in the annals of popular taste. One must give the sociologist's best and admit that *Goldfinger* really is rather a symbolic film.

critical responses   contexts

change in attitude

Houston may have been wrong in underestimating the films' longevity
and their continued relevance to audiences but her views are significant
because they mark a change in attitude to Bond: no longer just
entertainment but part of popular culture both in Britain and beyond.

bibliography

general film

Altman, Rick, *Film Genre*, BFI, 1999
Detailed exploration of the concept of film genre

Bordwell, David, *Narration in the Fiction Film*, Routledge, 1985
A detailed study of narrative theory and structures

– – –, Staiger, Janet & Thompson, Kristin, *The Classical Hollywood Cinema: Film Style & Mode of Production to 1960*, Routledge, 1985; pbk 1995
An authoritative study of cinema as institution, it covers film style and production

– – – & Thompson, Kristin, *Film Art*, McGraw-Hill, 4th edn, 1993
An introduction to film aesthetics for the non-specialist

Branson, Gill & Stafford, Roy, *The Media Student's Handbook*, Routledge, 2nd edn, 1999

Buckland, Warren, *Teach Yourself Film Studies*, Hodder & Stoughton, 1998
Very accessible, it gives an overview of key areas in film studies

Cook, Pam & Bernink, Mieke (eds), *The Cinema Book*, BFI, 2nd edn, 1999

Corrigan, Tim, *A Short Guide To Writing About Film*, HarperCollins, 1994
What it says: a practical guide for students

Dyer, Richard (with Paul McDonald), *Stars*, BFI, 2nd edn, 1998
A good introduction to the star system

Easthope, Antony, *Classical Film Theory*, Longman, 1993
A clear overview of writing about film theory

Hayward, Susan, *Key Concepts in Cinema Studies*, Routledge, 1996

Hill, John & Gibson, Pamela Church (eds), *The Oxford Guide to Film Studies*, Oxford University Press, 1998
Wide-ranging standard guide

Kennedy, Harlan, 'Kiltspotting: Highland Reels', in *Film Comment* vol.32 no.4, July-August 1996
An analysis of the style and themes of 1990s' Scottish films

Lapsley, Robert & Westlake, Michael, *Film Theory: An Introduction*, Manchester University Press, 1994

Maltby, Richard & Craven, Ian, *Hollywood Cinema*, Blackwell, 1995
A comprehensive work on the Hollywood industry and its products

McArthur, Colin, 'The Cultural Necessity of a Poor Celtic Cinema', in *Border Crossings: Film in Ireland, Britain and Europe*, John Hill, Martin McLoone and Paul Hainsworth (eds), BFI, 1994
A polemical argument about how Scottish cinema should be organised in order not to lose sight of specifically Scottish concerns

Mulvey, Laura, 'Visual Pleasure and Narrative Cinema' (1974), in *Visual and Other Pleasures*, Indiana University Press, Bloomington, 1989
The classic analysis of 'the look' and 'the male gaze' in Hollywood cinema. Also available in numerous other edited collections

Nelmes, Jill (ed.), *Introduction to Film Studies*, Routledge, 2nd edn, 1999
Deals with several national cinemas and key concepts in film study

Nowell-Smith, Geoffrey (ed.),
The Oxford History of World Cinema,
Oxford University Press, 1996
    Hugely detailed and wide-ranging
    with many features on 'stars'
**Roddick, Nick, 'Show Me the
Culture!',** in *Sight and Sound* vol.8
no.12, December 1998
    A polemical argument about the state
    of the British film industry in the late
    1990s and the type of film making
    this encourages
**Thomson, David, *A Biographical
Dictionary of the Cinema,***
Secker & Warburg, 1975
    Unashamedly driven by personal taste,
    but often stimulating
Truffaut, François, *Hitchcock,*
Simon & Schuster, 1966,
rev. edn. Touchstone, 1985
    Landmark extended interview
Turner, Graeme, *Film as Social Practice,*
3rd edn, Routledge, 1999

Chapter four, 'Film Narrative', discusses
structuralist theories of narrative
**Wollen, Peter, *Signs and Meaning in
the Cinema,*** BFI 1997 (revised edn)
    An important study in semiology

Readers should also explore the many
relevant websites and journals.
Film Education and *Sight and Sound*
are standard reading.
Valuable websites include:
The Internet Movie Database at
www.uk.imdb.com
Screensite at
www.tcf.ua.edu/screensite/contents.html
The Media and Communications Site
at the University of Aberystwyth at
www.aber.ac.uk/~dgc/welcome.html
There are obviously many other
university and studio websites which
are worth exploring in relation to film
studies.

goldfinger

Barber, Harry L., and Barber, Hoyt L.,
The Book of Bond, James Bond, Cyclone
books, 1999
    Useful for lots of facts and figures
**Barnes, Alan, and Hearn, Marcus, *Kiss
Kiss Bang! Bang!,*** Overlook Press, 1998
**Campbell, Joseph, *The Hero with a
Thousand Faces,*** Paladin Grafton, 1988
**Chapman, James, *Licence to Thrill: a
Cultural History of the James Bond
Films,*** Columbia University Press, 2000
    The most comprehensive and
    authoritative study of the Bond films
Lane, Andy, and Simpson, Paul,
The Bond Files, Virgin, 1998

Covers books, comics and incarnations
rather than just the films, useful but
limited.
Pfeiffer, Lee, and Worrall, Dave,
The Essential Bond,
Boxtree, 2000
**Rubin, Steven Jay, *The Complete
James Bond Movie Encyclopedia,***
Contemporary Books, 1995
    Very useful for finding out all sorts of
    information. Exhaustive.
Turner, Adrian, *Goldfinger,*
Bloomsbury, 1998
    Contains an excellent interview with
    Guy Hamilton

cinematic terms

classical narration the dominant form of film-making between 1930 and 1960, emphasising story-telling and plot over style

continuity editing unobtrusive editing designed to move from shot to shot without drawing attention to itself

diegetic describes the fictional world of the film's narrative (diegesis)

establishing shot a feature of continuity editing where a long shot establishes place and/or character before cutting to closer shots

German Expressionism a film movement which tried to make sets reflect emotional moods rather than reality

intercutting cutting between two shots or sequences in order to invite comparison and/or to indicate events happening simultaneously

low key/high key lighting low key lighting refers to low levels of light in a shot, sometimes with more than one source, and lots of shadows. High key lighting is an even bright light over a set

match on action when an action, e.g. walking, begins in one shot and continues over the cut into the next

mythic myth refers to any stories that try to explain a culture's basic beliefs about itself

POV a shot intended to be seen through the eyes or from the point of view of a particular character

rear projection an image is projected from behind on to a screen in front of which actors perform as the whole thing is refilmed

shot/reverse shot in a conversation between two people, after an establishing shot the first close up is called shot while the close up of the second person is called reverse because it is at the reverse end of an imaginary 180 degree line used in continuity editing

swish pan when the camera pans so rapidly the shot is blurred

tones tone refers to when one shade of colour dominates a scene

under cranking when film is shot at a slower speed than normal so that when it is played back at normal speed events will seem speeded up

vertical integration a term used to describe film studios' control of the means of production, distribution and exhibition

credits

production company
United Artists/Eon Productions

director
Guy Hamilton

producers
Albert R Broccoli and
Harry Salzman

screenplay
Richard Maibaum and Paul Dehn

**cinematographer/
director of photography**
Ted Moore

editor
Peter Hunt

production designer
Ken Adam

special effects
John Stears

main titles
Robert Brownjohn

music
John Barry

title song performed by
Shirley Bassey

lyrics
Leslie Bricusse, Anthony Newley

cast
James Bond – Sean Connery
Pussy Galore – Honor Blackman
Auric Goldfinger – Gert Frobe
Jill Masterson – Shirley Eaton
Oddjob – Harold Sakata
Tilly Masterson – Tania Mallet
M – Bernard Lee
Miss Moneypenny – Lois Maxwell
Q – Desmond Llewelyn